Zoar in the Civil War

Zoar in the Civil War

Philip E. Webber

❋ ❋ ❋

The Kent State University Press

Kent, Ohio

Library of Congress Catalog Card Number 2006028873

ISBN: 978-0-87338-906-8

Manufactured in the United States of America

11 10 09 08 07   5 4 3 2 1

Library of Congress Cataloging-in-Publication Data

Webber, Philip E., 1944–

Zoar in the Civil War / Philip E. Webber.

p.   cm.

Includes bibliographical references and index.

ISBN-13: 978-0-87338-906-8 (pbk. : alk. paper) ∞

ISBN-10: 0-87338-906-9 (pbk. : alk. paper) ∞

1. Society of Separatists of Zoar—History.

2. United States—History—Civil War, 1861–1865.

I. Title.

HX656.Z8W43 2007

973.7'1—dc22   2006028873

British Library Cataloging-in-Publication data are available.

Contents

Acknowledgments

It is a joy to thank all whose advice and encouragement contributed to this study. Kathleen Fernandez, former site director of Zoar Village State Memorial, offered key insights and information. Steve Shonk, also at Zoar Village, provided help early in my research. So many individuals in the archives and library of the Ohio Historical Society came to my assistance that I wish to express my gratitude to the entire staff, particularly those whose efforts went beyond expectation: Betsy Butler, Cynthia Ghering, and Elizabeth L. Plummer. Central College provided welcome research and development funds, and I gladly thank all my colleagues there, as well as friends in the Amana Colonies and colleagues in the Communal Studies Association, for uplifting words at just the right moments. The Ohio Historical Society and the Western Reserve Historical Society generously granted permission to quote from their archival material; Mark Gaynor of Indian River Graphics in Zoar, Ohio, granted permission to quote from Jacob Smith's *Camps and Campaigns of the 107th Regiment Ohio Volunteer Infantry, from August, 1862, to July, 1865*. Only after I began this research did I realize that Zoar's history captured the long-term interest of the late Elmer Zollinger, who had already influenced me and my thinking in so many ways. More than anyone else, however, I owe a debt of gratitude to my wife, Janice, to whom I gladly dedicate this book.

An Overview of Zoar
in the Civil War

The Society of Separatists of Zoar was exactly what it claimed to be: a group of immigrants from Germany that eschewed religious ceremonies, had severed ties with the Württemberg state church, and, under the leadership of Josef (Joseph) Michael Bäumeler (also Bäumler, later Bimeler), had migrated to the United States.[1] From 1817 to 1898, the Separatists existed as a Pietist communal society in Tuscarawas County, Ohio.[2] Zoar—named for the town where Lot found refuge when the Lord destroyed Sodom and Gomorrah—ranks among the longest-lived single-site communitarian experiments in American history.[3]

Terms such as "separatist" and "communal" may foster notions of self-sufficient isolationism. Such was not quite the case. The community paid off its initial debt for some 5,000 acres of land by contracting to build part of the Ohio & Erie Canal; it enjoyed brisk commerce in manufactured goods and agricultural products over a considerable geographic area; and it earned a reputation for shrewd, if nonetheless scrupulously honest, capitalism and entrepreneurial acumen.

Zoar operated a large and well-known hotel (opened in 1833) in response to the needs of the community's business clientele and a growing tourism industry. It is no accident that there exists an extensive photographic documentation of life in Zoar, for while some members of the Society complained from time to time about the rigors imposed by a thriving tourism industry, there never existed any *policy* as such of trying to keep non-Zoarites out of the community, including those who appeared on-site with cameras in hand.

Thanks to the rich and abundant selection of images that has been preserved, Zoar Village State Memorial's former site director, Kathleen M.

Zoar as it appeared toward the end of the communal era, in an aerial view taken from the Zoar Hotel tower. Photo courtesy of Ohio Historical Society.

Fernandez, has been able to publish *A Singular People: Images of Zoar.* With its extensive commentaries, this volume is more than an anthology of historic photographs: it is also the best current resource for the study of Zoar's social history and probably the first volume that a serious scholar should consult before embarking on a research program involving the Zoar community.[4]

Consistent with all this is the fact that Zoar enjoyed coverage in a number of both prominent and lesser-known nineteenth- and early-twentieth-century publications.[5] Although these accounts were based on personal contact with America's communal societies, in certain areas the Society of Separatists had no intention of conforming to the pattern of the outside world. In the sectarian literature of the community, frequent mention is made of the "Principles of Separatism" (die Grundsätze des Separatismus), and it is not always clear in a given text whether the author is referring to the general ideological underpinnings of Zoar's Pietism or to the clearly expressed Twelve Principles.

In summary, these principles included faith in a triune God, affirmation that humanity lost its likeness to God through the fall of Adam, belief in a restored relationship with God through Christ, acceptance of Holy Scripture as life's guide and standard against which to judge all things, rejection of religious ceremonies as meaningless and indeed injurious to true spirituality, avoidance of speech or gestures that accord mortals the honor that is due to God alone (this included exclusive use of the informal German pronoun *du*), denunciation of ecclesiastical regulations that promote sectarianism, marriage by mutual consent before witnesses and with subsequent notification of civil authorities but without services of the clergy, recognition of total chastity as the better way and of sexual intercourse as sinful when not engaged in to propagate the race, refusal to send children to "the schools of Babylon" (i.e., to schools whose curricula represented the intertwined interests of church and state), and obedience, insofar as possible, to civil authorities.

The remaining principle, eleventh on the original list, dealt with the bearing of arms: "We cannot serve the state as bodily soldiers, since a Christian cannot murder his enemy, much less his friend."[6] The writings of the Zoar Separatists make clear their assumption that soldiers are trained to kill, if so commanded, and that a soldier who pledges allegiance to his superiors has, in effect, consented to killing as an act that he is prepared to carry out.

Historically speaking, this principle involved more than simply a philosophical or ideological rationale for espousing a particular stance in the debate on the proper regard for human life. Having "come out of Babylon" in Germany, where records of membership in the state church, of citizenship, and—for males—of preregistration for military induction were well-nigh inseparable, refusing military service in the European homeland had constituted a powerful political expression of the separatism embraced by these resilient, radical Pietists.[7] Having at times paid the price of physical abuse and incarceration for their pacifist ideals, the Separatists were not inclined to yield readily to pressures favoring compromise. How did it happen, then, in the context of this staunchly pacifist tradition, that four of the five Civil War veterans proudly wearing the medals of the Grand Army of the Republic in the photo below are from Zoar?

In the United States, a new ingredient came into the mix: slavery, an institution vehemently opposed by the vast majority of German Americans and by the Pietists in Zoar.[8] In Ohio, the Germans' abolitionist stance typically expressed itself in a prompt response by young men to the call for volunteers in the Union forces. Among the state's units in which German American soldiers distinguished themselves were (to name but a few) the

This portrait of Civil War veterans from Zoar, Ohio, identifies the subjects as "Harry Bowman (Cleveland), Leo Kern (boss over teamsters), John Kuecherer [Kücherer] (baker), D. Unsold (left Society), Anton Burkhart (brewmaster)." The medals indicate membership in the Grand Army of the Republic, an organization for Union veterans. Photo courtesy of Ohio Historical Society.

9th (Cincinnati's famous Neuner), 28th, 37th, 106th, and 107th Ohio Volunteer Infantries.[9] No doubt these German American soldiers would have been gratified to know that Germans on the continent would continue over the years to be proud of them for the stance they took. It would also have pleased them to know that their distant relatives would be as interested in the circumstances of the common man as in the achievements of prominent officers. These German American soldiers could not have known, of course, that one day some of the most detailed Web sites on their role in the Civil War would be maintained by individuals and organizations located in the European homeland.[10]

What action did the Separatists of Zoar take in response to the Civil War, and to the social and political issues that caused it? Surprisingly little information appears in E. O. Randall's otherwise foundational study, pub-

lished only a few years after formal dissolution of Zoar as a communal society. Edgar B. Nixon's 1933 doctoral dissertation at Ohio State University
presents only a succinct—albeit important—overview of activity in Zoar
during the Civil War. But until now, popular perceptions of how Zoar
experienced the American Civil War have tended to be formed by Janet
Hickman's historical novel *Zoar Blue,* first published in 1978 and reprinted
in a limited edition for the Ohio Historical Society in 1998. In the author's
note, Hickman explains that "except for [the fictitious Zoar soldier] John
Keffer and [non-Zoarite sidekick Isaac] Braunmiller, who is also an inven-
tion, the names given [in *Zoar Blue*] are those of real people."[11] In many
ways, Keffer and Braunmiller are undeniably credible composite portraits
of Civil War soldiers from Zoar and the surrounding area. Their experiences recall historically verifiable events. Names in the novel such as Brunny, Kern, Unseldt, Wright, Kücherer, Rieker, Geissler, Burkhart, Zeib, Kappel (and their orthographic variants) appear in the roster of Zoarites who
entered the Union forces.[12] Hickman has obviously done her research.

All this may lead to the impression that *Zoar Blue,* while an admittedly
captivating narrative, is also objective historical scholarship. Though one
may concede that, in overall tone, the novel is strikingly consonant with
the extant record, it is not—nor was it intended primarily to be—a factual
account of how Zoar experienced the Civil War. But what is the extant
record that might enrich our understanding of this topic? At this point, it
consists in great part of unpublished primary sources. The purpose of the
present study is to allow those sources to speak for themselves, and in so
doing, to stimulate still further inquiry.

The Ohio Historical Society owns several manuscript collections dedi-
cated to the history of Zoar, the most undisputedly comprehensive being the Society of Separatists of Zoar Records, 1811–1946 (1816–1942).[13]
Additional unpublished material on Zoar during the Civil War includes
the important but understudied component of the Nixon Family Papers
at the Ohio Historical Society.[14] The most important untapped source of
information on the present topic, however, is the Jack and Pat Adamson
Collection, a corpus of primary materials that significantly expands our
understanding of Zoar during the communal era, including the 1860s.
Most Civil War–era correspondence cited in this study is drawn from the
Adamson Collection.[15] One final source of primary documentation is the
collection of papers and photographic images from Zoar at the Western
Reserve Historical Society in Cleveland, Ohio.[16] This cache of materials is

primarily—though not exclusively—important for understanding the economic history of the Society of Separatists of Zoar during the Civil War.[17]

Except as otherwise indicated, those original documents written by and for members of the Zoar community are in German, and I have provided the translation.[18] In some of the material originally written in English (primarily documents intended for an outside readership), I have made minor corrections in spelling and punctuation where doing so aids clarity without changing the substantive content of the document or masking the character of the text.

In the aggregate, the Zoarites were literate and well informed. A letter by Christian Weebel (earlier Wiebel) dated October 16, 1867, includes an order for school materials. Unfortunately, there is no similar document from Zoar in the Civil War period, but Weebel's evident familiarity with the requested materials suggests that this list of books might not differ a great deal from one that might have been compiled just a few years earlier, during the actual period of the Civil War. At any rate, the books show that the Zoar school curriculum was certainly more than adequate for its time.

30 Wilson's Primary Spellers
24 Copybooks each, Nos. 1, 2, 3, 4 and 5
24 Pinneo's revised and enlarged primary Grammars
40 Ray's Arithmetics [sic], 3rd Part
24 Eclectic Spellers (McDuffie's [sic] if to be had handily)
 6 Lippincott's primary Geographies[19]

In addition, the Zoar schools used various books designed for a German American audience. By this period, however, education in German was already in decline in the Zoar classroom.

Records of the post office in Zoar present an impressive list of published material, in both German and English, received by the Society itself and by individuals (both members and non-members) living there.[20] Topics covered during the period of the Civil War included politics, agriculture, religion, finance, and education. Notices of newspapers and magazines received from Cincinnati, Cleveland, Pittsburgh, and Philadelphia appear regularly in the postmaster's record.

On May 31, 1861, in response to a letter of inquiry written two days earlier by Zoar's David Silvan, Henry Andermann (a frequent business partner and personal associate of the Zoarites), of New Philadelphia, Ohio, listed German newspapers published in Cincinnati, noting their political leanings but disclaiming detailed familiarity with any of them.[21] Andermann suggests that Silvan write to the publishers and request sample issues. The papers listed are the Republican *Volksblatt, Republikaner, Hochwächter,* and *Turnerzeitung,* the Democrat *Volksfreund,* and the Catholic *Wahrheitsfreund.*

On July 25, 1862, publisher and bookseller Ignaz Kohler, of Philadelphia, who regularly supplied the Society with reading material, sent sample copies of six different newspapers to Zoar. In an accompanying letter in German to David Silvan, a certain Martin Kohler noted that "the Philadelphia newspapers do not have the best reputation, as they never have much [significant] reading matter. If you want to take any, take the *Republikanische Flagge,* which I consider the best. It remains the most consistent, though as a matter of principle, I do not want to preempt your choice, and no doubt you will do just fine in making a decision. There are two daily and four weekly papers, and they all state their prices. If you decide on one or the other, just write to [our] office for punctual service."[22] Kohler closes with greetings to another member of the Zoar community with whom he had had previous contact. If one thing is clear from the tone of his letter, it is that Kohler assumed he was dealing with readers whose stance of separation was one of informed choice rather than one of indifference to, or ignorance of, current events.

Although it is unlikely that the Zoar community had much direct contact with African Americans, Hilda Dischinger Morhart's *The Zoar Story* tells of longtime hired laborer Jacob Lubold, who discovered a runaway slave hiding in some hay pitched the previous day from the loft of a community barn.[23] Though evidently an isolated instance, this one surely enjoyed eager circulation, perhaps even embellishment, as it was recounted in various social circles in and around Zoar. Moreover, considering Zoar's location between lines of the Underground Railroad, the story is not at all implausible.[24]

Another account preserved by Morhart tells of how Union soldier John Kücherer was trapped under a heavy timber. Just when he was about to give up hope, a black man rescued him. According to Morhart, Kücherer continued for the rest of his life to recount this tale and to express his gratitude to his unknown black benefactor.[25] Lubold and Kücherer may have been among the few Zoarites to have seen a black person in such close proximity.

· · ·

During and after the conflict of 1861–65, residents in Zoar owned various books on American history in general, and specifically on the Civil War. Jonathan Breymaier (Breymeier), born in 1852 and a mere lad when the Civil War broke out, owned a compilation of German works, bound into a single volume, into which he entered his name on March 23, 1866. The first part is a moralizing tract on the dangers of riches and power, illustrated by the rise and fall of Alexander Menshikov, the companion of Peter the Great, who was later exiled to Siberia; the second is the account of a German American Union soldier stationed in Virginia; the third deals with the capture of a white person by the Indians.[26] It is tempting to picture the parents of the Zoarite youth who read this book, gratified by their son's interest in a didactic tract on the perils of materialism, when in fact little Jonathan was absorbing the thrilling accounts of heroic soldiers and of dangers faced in the confrontations between Indians and white settlers. At this point, the imaginative scholar needs to beware of creating historical fiction, or even fictitious history. What may reasonably be supposed, however, is that tales purporting to convey the romance and adventure of America's tragic Civil War were not altogether lacking an audience among Zoar's young readers. At a later period, Jacob Dischinger (1871–1958) owned a German translation of John S. C. Abbott's history of the Civil War in America.[27] It would be interesting to know whether Dischinger was the first owner of this work, and if not, who first purchased it, when, and out of what motivation.

Excellent insights into the Separatists' awareness of events in Washington, D.C., and on the battlefield come from the daybooks and annotated account records of the Civil War era. The most complete such work is the journal maintained by Simon Beuter (Beiter).[28] Born in 1819 at Bietenhausen, Germany, Beuter immigrated to the United States in 1840, with Zoar as his destination. Three brothers and his parents eventually followed. Beuter formally joined the Separatists in 1843.

Simon Beuter worked as a gardener (as did Josef M. Bäumeler), served as a school teacher, and was without doubt the most comprehensive chronicler of life in Zoar as well as the recognized standard-bearer for the use of cultivated and correct German. As late as 1932, one individual could recall Beuter insisting on the use of standard German and discouraging the use of provincialisms. German is a language whose spelling is far more phonetic than that of English, and the redoubtable Beuter showed little inhibition about telling an individual who spoke with a strong regional accent to "Buchstabiere das!" (Spell it!) as a way of helping the hapless lin-

The Zoar garden existed as early as 1829. Among Society members who maintained the garden was Simon Beuter, to whom the garden owes much of its form. Various interpretations exist for the items in the garden and their configuration. Photo courtesy of Ohio Historical Society.

guistic transgressor to recognize and correct any faults in pronunciation.[29] An overview of topics treated in Beuter's journal, supplemented by information from other sources of the period, affords a unique and surprisingly detailed overview of Zoar during the Civil War.

January 1860: Congress has been in Washington for six weeks but cannot get organized. Seemingly all that appears certain is that slavery is a blot of shame (ein Schandfleck) that cannot be allowed to stay.

June 1860: In both Europe and America, the fires of war are ready to burst into flames. The Society of Separatists of Zoar is faring no better than others: it seems that everyone is prepared to find fault with others, but not with oneself.

November 1860: On the 6th of the month, the presidential election passes without incident; Republican candidate Abraham Lincoln wins by "an enormous majority" (eine ungeheure Mehrheit).

The man supervising garden work in this photo is probably Simon Beuter. Photo courtesy of Ohio Historical Society.

January 1861: Only the sword appears capable of settling the dispute between North and South over the issue of slavery. The insanity of the slaveholders (die Verrücktheit der Sklawenhalter) leaves no room for compromise, and "the North is not going to give up any of its rights, nor should it."

February 1861: South Carolina, Georgia, Florida, Alabama, and Louisiana secede from the Union. From the South comes nothing but violence and betrayal. The journal keeper Simon Beuter rebukes President Buchanan's perceived ineptitude.

April 1861: Despite the depressing likelihood of war in the South and abroad, there is still cause to rejoice: the outlook for Zoar's fruit crop remains favorable. In the face of war between the government and the rebel slaveholders, the plausibility of revolution increases. Virginia has seceded from the Union. Beuter offers various comments on Alexander II of Russia, the papacy, and Napoleon III. The president has requested 300,000 troops.

May 1861: To date, 81,000 volunteer troops have enlisted in Ohio.

July 1861: On Independence Day, Congress meets to discuss the war. For a week or so prior to that time, a (possibly portentous?) comet has been seen in the northern heavens. Later in the month, the president requests $400,000,000 and 400,000 troops to put down the conspiracy (um die Verschwörung zu unterdrücken); it is noted later in the month that Congress has in fact granted the president $500,000,000 and 500,000 troops. How blessed is the Union, says Beuter, and how sad the state of the South! Losses are reported for the first Battle of Bull Run/Manassas.

Meanwhile, still other members of the Zoar community noted with concern the seeming inevitability of war. In a letter dated January 3, 1861, Jacob Silvan (Jakob Sylvan) expressed his anxieties to R. L. Baker at the Economy communal society.[30] As Kathleen Fernandez has noted, this was one of only a few rare instances in which communication between such communal groups included mention of current events.[31]

Given the mood and the level of information current in Zoar around the time of the Civil War, it was but a matter of time until conflict emerged between the Separatists' conscientious objection to war and their ideological impulse toward conscientious participation in what they considered to be the just cause of the Union.

By September 1861 the time for decision had arrived. With seeming surprise, Simon Beuter noted in his journal entry for that month, "The worst thing about the war, as far as our Society is concerned, is that seven of our youth, some of them still underage lads, have allowed themselves to be recruited. This is in direct opposition to our principles, and shows that they have not yet made the Principles of Separatism their own. Our forebears suffered for these very same principles until they prevailed. Three of these volunteers were taken back because they had not yet reached the necessary age, one withdrew of his own accord, and one no longer had any desire and took off [machte sich aus dem Staub]; there are now two still in the army who came directly from our Society."

The cash books show that the Society gave each of the departing recruits $2 on September 7, 1861, thus indicating that the would-be enlistment of 1861 was an act discussed at least to some extent between the young men and their fellow Zoarites. Unfortunately, the account books give only the family names of the recruits: "Beeler, Kücherer, Kern, Miller, Rieker, Knöpfle." (The seventh was Simon Breil.) Although one may presume the identity of these recruits from various other records, there is also a degree of uncertainty in some instances about just which member of a given family may have been involved. At any rate, two days later, on September 9, 1861, the cash books mention "Beeler, Kücherer, Kern & Rieker" as having made "their return from C[anal] Dover to this place" and as having thereupon returned their cash advances.[32] This seems to indicate that recruit Miller had indeed enlisted, but that is not quite the entire story. In a letter dated September 8, 1861, Michael Miller explained to R. L. Baker at the Economy communal society what had transpired with his son, Christian Miller.

> Dear Friend Baker,
> Circumstances force me to write you a few lines. The person bringing this letter to you is my son. He committed an error in my absence by becoming a volunteer soldier, along with others. They were not all yet adults and could get free from the recruit- ers, who have no right to recruit minors. We could also obtain my son's freedom because it could be shown that the recruiters almost forced them to sign, though [our action] was complicated and gave the Society a bad name [und die Gesellschaft auch dadurch belästigt (wurde)]. And he himself regretted it and told me he would leave himself. [Was Christian Miller the one who "no longer had any de- sire and took off"?] So his mother and I have given him the advice to go to you, which he willingly accepted, though he wishes that none would know where he is. I gladly agreed to this, for my conscience does not [allow me to] permit him to become a solider if he regrets [having taken that step].[33]

The elder Miller then goes on to make special requests regarding work and housing for his son, whom he appears to view as a rather tender lad, and to mention that (Jacob) Silvan had given each of the young men some money upon their departure from Zoar. Christian Miller, who did not return his cash to the Zoar coffers, intended to use the money to travel to Economy. Michael Miller frankly admits that for this reason he finds it awkward to discuss his son's case with the Society leadership.

J. C. Haring, of Massillon, Ohio, was the photographer who created this cabinet card portrait of Michael Miller, probably during the 1880s. Miller was the last living Separatist who emigrated directly from Germany to Zoar. Photo courtesy of Ohio Historical Society.

In his final entry for 1861, Beuter identifies the two Zoarite soldiers who did in fact remain in military service as Simon Breil (not mentioned in the cash books cited above) and Samuel Knöpfle (Knoeffle, Knopfly), who both served in Company B of the 51st Ohio Volunteer Infantry.[34] Since their unit was organized at Canal Dover, Ohio, these first Zoarite volunteers were recruited from under the noses, as it were, of the Society leadership. Beuter mentions in his year-end comments for 1861 that the two had left the Society, presumably of their own volition rather than under discipline for having enlisted (although that point is not entirely clear). Be that as it may, Breil and Knöpfle returned to Zoar after the conflict and appear in later records as members of the Society, working respectively as a tanner and as a tailor. As for Christian Miller, he returned to Zoar and on April 11, 1862, Jacob Silvan mentioned in a letter to R. L. Baker at Economy that, as far as he was concerned, "Christian Miller had meanwhile devoted himself so much to military affairs" that Miller's assignment in Zoar of printing books "was probably a lost cause."[35]

Simon Beuter, meanwhile, despite claims that volunteer enlistment was "the worst thing about the war as far as our Society is concerned," continued to follow the course of the war with unabashedly keen interest. Modern readers who do not know that Beuter was an avowed pacifist might detect something almost exultant in the tone in which he enumerates the details of victories scored by the Union. In January 1862 Beuter reports—with apparent admiration—the victories of Cincinnati's famous German Neuner (9th Ohio Volunteer Infantry). In February he praises the troops under German-born Gen. Franz Sigel (also Siegel, 1824–1902), who "cleaned the rebels out of Missouri." March includes a vignette on the headway made by Gen. Ambrose Everett Burnside. For each month, there is some update, and often there are several, on the main events of the war. Invariably, Beuter takes the stance of an unyielding supporter of the Union cause, and as one not altogether shy about expressing open delight in the German American contributions to the war effort.

For July 1862 (between a lament over the fate of America's blossoming manhood being subjected to wartime death and disease and speculation on possible consequences of European intervention in the war) is the fateful observation by Beuter that a shortfall of volunteers to supply the projected need of 300,000 additional Union troops would necessitate a system of selection by lot. Beuter failed to recognize—or perhaps simply chose to ignore in the entries of his journal—impending signs that Zoar was about to see some one dozen young men volunteer for military service. Zoar did in fact have to deal eventually with the consequences of a lot-based draft system but in the meantime needed to come to terms with a more immediate problem.

The next major event in the story of Zoar in the war begins with an unsigned statement dated August 1, 1862. The unidentified author expresses his inner urgency to find a practical expression for his patriotic impulses. The style is reminiscent of the writings of Eugene B. Wright, whose correspondence and other writings will be considered later in this study.

Esteemed Friend!

Because our oppressed fatherland must presently offer almost every possible means to suppress this rebellion, along with all the evil that it brings, I likewise consider it my duty to contribute something to the rapid alleviation of the oppression.[36] For I cannot nonchalantly watch the destruction of our fatherland, purchased at such a dear price, without also attempting to uphold our free laws, Constitution, and rights, so blessed in their impact upon the people of this land and won by the patriotic blood of our forebears.

Were I to attempt to justify myself in response to the question, "What have you done to suppress the rebellion and to effect restoration of a joyous peace?" my truthful answer would have to be: Nothing.

To the question, "Do you consider yourself a patriot?" the answer is: Yes.

"Wherein does your patriotism consist?" In recognition of the laws and government.

"Does this entitle you to the weighty name of a *PATRIOT*?" How could I defend myself? As one who thanklessly enjoys our free rights, and as an idle participant in the fate of my fatherland and of my fellow man, [as one] whose only effort is to feather his own nest [seinen eigenen Sack zu spicken] while his fellow man stands prepared to sacrifice almost everything, even his most beloved *life,* in order to remove this baleful fate as quickly as possible, would it be possible for me to justify myself? No!

Therefore, I have decided to do something that might be beneficial to restoration of peace. For I feel within me the duty to support the benefits gained at such a price by our forefathers, those that God has allowed us to enjoy for such a long time and in undisturbed peace, and that have brought a joyous fortune to all.

Should we watch with folded hands as robbers and murderers destroy these benefits and abuse the noble and free rights of humanity while hundreds of innocent persons must offer everything, including their own lives?

All this is due to the diabolic bloodlust of traitors to the most blessed government on earth. Through his grace, God bequeathed all this to our forefathers—they being worthy of such fortune—in compensation for the costly loss of that which had been *most precious* to them in their battle for freedom. This was to show his mighty arm to the rest of the world. For had it not been his express will, our forefathers would have been unable to wrest their freedom under such circumstances as those in which they found themselves.

Who would have believed that God appointed this beneficent system of freedom only to have it last so short a time? Not I! I do believe, however, that this rebellion and the resultant hard times are the consequence of our people's ingratitude toward the kind Giver of these benefits. There needs to be a restoration of the people to the earlier unity and mutual love between brother and sister, so that we might, more than ever, call upon the only Helper to lead us to a destiny where brother-blood will cease to flow.

This will come about after this terrible rebellion—perpetrated by these most gruesome individuals who have set aside all love of fellow man—has been put down. This is something that we can only bring about by the strict arm of justice and the help of God—something that we cannot do except through mighty support of a government that uses every means to suppress this malevolent rebellion!

Let us now decide by what means we can best contribute to this cause. We must act, for God has richly supplied us with the means necessary to do so. Since he has granted us these means, should we allow them to lie unused? No! Let us rather attempt all that lies within our power, and at the same time, let us call upon him to share his all-enabling blessing with us. For without his help, our most zealous efforts are in vain.

Through intense intercession and a change of our former way of life, this will be granted, for we know, [in allusion to Psalm 22:5–7 and similar Biblical passages] "Those who call upon the name of the Lord will not come to shame!" Now let us take counsel as to what will be best for us, and then act accordingly, with the concurrence of our friends, and with the sole intention of fulfilling our duty to God and to our country.

To God, we say, because it is he who has afforded us all these benefits, and certainly not just to see them destroyed so soon; to our fellow humans, in order to protect them from something still more dire. For those unable to fight for such benefits, let us send ourselves into the unavoidable fray, be it ever so arduous, and offer our every power to suppress this terrible rebellion in the shortest time possible.[37]

Unfortunately, the essay breaks off at the top of the fourth page, just at the moment when the reader is prepared for a statement supporting conscientious participation in, rather than conscientious objection to, active military service in the Civil War. Definite identification of the Zoarite who authored this text is also lacking.[38] Obviously, the individual who drafted this statement was far from alone in his sentiments. Within the month, there appeared an undated statement by the young men from Zoar who had decided to enlist in the Union army in the late summer of 1862.

The undersigned wish to let you know herewith that they intend soon to leave for Cleveland, Ohio, in order to enter the German regiment there . . . [though] we would not have decided to take this step if it could have been avoided. However, since soon there will be a lottery, we wish to enlist now. We know that it is contrary to the Principles of the Separatists to go to war, but now, in this present crisis, in order to contend for freedom and human rights, we feel it our duty to unite our forces with those who, at the first call, sacrifice all, indeed their most precious lives, in order to contend on behalf of those who cannot fight for posterity and for a free home. We await an approval or rejection of our appeal.
Signed with greatest amicability, [no signatures on this sole extant copy].[39]

"We await an approval or rejection of our appeal" suggests that this document might have circulated prior to departure for Cleveland. If, according to a local legend discussed below, the young men stole off to enlist, then perhaps this statement was left behind as an explanation of measures taken by the new recruits. Either way, the course of action was taken after significant deliberation. Aware of the impending draft lottery, these men chose to take matters into their own hands. It is worth suggesting that the decision not to wait for selection by lot may have arisen from more than patriotic impulse alone. Perhaps these recruits-by-choice foresaw the difficulty that older community leaders would later have in coping with the draft and its ramifications, and they consequently determined not to entrust their fate to those whose insights and experiences were so different from their own.

In contrast to one year earlier, Beuter made no direct mention in his journal of the 1862 voluntary enlistment when it took place, and after the fact only obliquely. However, there was no lack of official reaction by the Society of Separatists to this second wave of response by its young men to the desperate pleas of the Union for fresh personnel in its armed forces.

Hilda Dischinger Morhart, in *The Zoar Story*, lists the names of those who reportedly stole off into the night in order to enlist in the Union army.[40] Morhart suggests that this may not have been an entirely clandestine scheme, since each recruit is supposed to have taken along a handwritten copy of Psalm 91, prepared by a mother, sister, or sweetheart and intended to be worn at all times to protect its bearer from harm.[41] One can readily imagine the comfort from passages in this psalm (presumably in their German version), such as, "Thou shalt not be afraid for the terror by night; nor for the arrow that flieth by day" (verse 5), "A thousand shall fall at thy side, and ten thousand at thy right hand; but it shall not come nigh thee" (verse 7), "For he shall give his angels charge over thee, to keep thee in all thy ways" (verse 11), or "Because he hath set his love upon me, therefore will I deliver him: I will set him on high, because he hath known my name" (verse 14).

In her section on the Civil War, Morhart also recounts various individual wartime experiences, including those transmitted orally in the Zoar community concerning Leo Kern, imprisoned at Andersonville; Anton Burkhart, who saw President Lincoln; and John Kücherer, rescued by an African American from under a fallen piece of timber. All three of these men appear, incidentally, in the picture of Zoar veterans wearing the medal of the Grand Army of the Republic. These may have been exactly the men whose pride in their own service contributed most to the perpetuation of a local memory of Zoar's role in the Civil War.

Morhart commemorates the courage of hired laborer Jacob Lubold in the face of the Morgan's raid scare, and she documents the tradition of an unnamed clairvoyant cabinetmaker who claimed to have experienced séances with the spirit of a departed Indian who "reported" the Battle of

Gettysburg and the assassination of Lincoln before official news reached Zoar. [42] While one may question the factual nature of some information in Morhart's *The Zoar Story,* it would be unwise to discount too quickly the material she presents. It is, after all, the best available record of what members of the Zoar community chose to perpetuate in their own traditional accounts.

Except for those who had in fact *already* enlisted in 1861, the men in Morhart's list were assigned to Company I of the 107th Ohio Volunteer Infantry; they officially entered the armed forces on August 22, 1862, were mustered in on September 9 of that year, and, except for death or incapacity, were mustered out on July 10, 1865.[43] These soldiers, cited with their ages upon enlistment and some common variant surname forms, were Simon Breil, who enlisted at age 20 in 1861; John Brunny (Brunne), 22; Anton (Anthony) Burkhart, 22; John Geissler (Geißler), 21; Gottfried Kappel, 22; Leo Kern, 20; Samuel Knöffle, who enlisted at age 22 in 1861; John Kücherer (Kuecherer), 19; Christian Rieker (Riker), 20; Franz (Frank) Strobel, 22; Daniel Unsöld (Unseldt, Unsold), 25; Eugene B. Wright, 20; and Adam (John A.?) Zeib (Zeeb), 18.[44]

There were still others. In 1995 Donna DeBlasio, then with the Ohio Historical Society, combined census information, the records of the database of persons associated with the Zoar community, and other resources to provide a much more detailed and complete list.[45] In 1998 Steve Shonk added personal and family background on some of the soldiers for an article in the *Zoar Star.*[46] For those interested primarily in family and personal histories, the results of DeBlasio's and Shonk's research may be of particular interest.

One might guardedly expand the list of veterans by adding the following names, though the exact nature of any connection between some of these men and the Zoar community is less clear. Their enlistment spans the years 1862–64: John Breil, 23[47]; Magnus (Magnes) Burkhart (Burghart), 20[48]; John Jähle (Jahle, Jähly), age uncertain[49]; Frederick Kücherer, 21[50]; George Kuemmele (Kümmerle), 21[51]; Jacob Kuemmerle (Kümmerle), 23[52]; John Kuemmerle (Kümmerle), 18[53]; Huldreich Langlotz, age uncertain[54]; John Smith, 24[55]; Lucas Strobel, 19[56]; and Jacob Thumm, 18.[57] Conceivably, as many as two dozen soldiers with a tie to Zoar may have served in the Union forces.

These men from Zoar were diverse in several ways. DeBlasio's and Shonk's research efforts and material from the soldiers' own letters reveal that a wide variety of trades were represented by the Zoarite soldiers, perhaps especially so since many men in Zoar worked in more than one capacity before settling in at a single work station.[58] There were farm laborers (as were virtually all able-bodied Zoarites at some point), a tanner, a brewer, a tailor, a blacksmith, a printer's apprentice, a shoemaker, and more. Five died while in active service (John Breil, Gottfried Kappel, Jacob and John Kümmerle, and Lucas Strobel).[59] One returned to Zoar to die of tuberculosis (Eugene B. Wright). Two served as military musicians (John Brunny and Huldreich Langlotz).[60] At least two were married (Huldreich Langlotz and Franz Strobel). Franz Strobel attained the rank of sergeant July 1, 1863, and Daniel Unsöld that of corporal July 1, 1863. Eugene B. Wright was reduced in rank from sergeant to private December 1, 1862; he was suffering health problems at the time of his demotion in rank, but other factors may possibly have played a role as well. Leo Kern spent months in the notorious Andersonville Prison, though little survives in the written record of that episode in the Civil War experience of the soldiers from Zoar.[61] According to Morhart, Kern was captured when he returned from flight to reclaim a fallen knapsack. After returning to Zoar, he would recount the horrors of the prison and how some starving and desperate prisoners would breach the rules of the prison in order to be shot and thereby put out of their misery.[62]

It is noteworthy that those soldiers who enlisted in the late summer of 1862 were mostly above the minimum age and thus perhaps motivated by different impulses than the youngest would-be recruits of 1861. The cash books for the period beginning August 1862 show that several of these men (or their family or friends) deposited money to be kept during their absence. Over the course of the war, many sent money home for deposit or used the general accounts of the Society to conduct transactions. (Even bounty money was handled via the general account of the Society.[63]) The recruits of August 1862 did not enlist on a whim and evidently anticipated service that might extend over a considerable period of time.

This undated autobiographical statement of Eugene B. Wright (1842–64) offers the most telling account of the initial experiences of these volunteers. (Wright's count of nine others beside himself is at variance with most records.)

> After the harvest I helped again in the Store until nine others and I entered the army on August 21, 1862. On the 25th of the month,

Fieldwork was demanding but also socially stimulating. Here we see workers in something approaching parade formation. Photo courtesy of Ohio Historical Society.

we left our home and were sent to Cleveland, Ohio, to enter camp there, where we arrived in the evening. After about one month, we received marching orders to go to Kentucky. We left Cleveland September 21, 9:00 A.M., and arrived the same day in Cincinnati at 8:00 P.M. There we received our frugal evening meal consisting of good bread, bacon, onions, and coffee, which was very welcome to us since it also had to do as our lunch. After we had strengthened ourselves once again, we went over the Ohio River to Covington, Kentucky, where, after unnecessarily marching around for a while, we set up our campsite at a place called Park. This was without rugs or tents, which we received only the next day. The 23rd we once again received marching orders and thereupon marched a long detour to Camp . . . , about a mile and a half south of Cincinnati.

We stayed there about ten days. Once, at about 3:00 A.M., we had to go to the trenches until about 6:00 A.M. because there was fear of a surprise attack that did not, however, take place. After some ten days, we were ordered back to Camp Delaware, Ohio, where the Regiment stayed about three weeks.[64]

The new inductees doubtless knew that they were joining a German regiment (the 107th Ohio Voluntary Infantry) in Cleveland.[65] Jacob Smith, a veteran of this regiment, makes special mention in his memoir, *Camps and Campaigns*, of the successful appeal of recruiters to young German American men, not least of all because of the success—albeit disputed by some—of German-born Gen. Franz Sigel, whose visibility was enhanced by "I am Going to Fight Mit Sigel" (or some variation thereupon), a song set to the tune of "The Girl I Left Behind" and sung widely through-out the Union forces.[66] While it is not known whether the "Sigel factor" played any direct role in initially attracting young Zoarites, several of them later mention Sigel in their letters home. It would be ironic if the pacifistic Simon Beuter, in the evident esteem of Sigel as a military leader (reflected in his journal entries), were in fact praising the very man whose person contributed to the recruitment of young men from Zoar.

Jacob Smith, who spoke only English, tells of several considerations given to the German Americans who constituted the majority of his regiment. Most church services, for example, were conducted in German.[67] There is also at least some evidence suggesting that Zoar's soldiers formed friendships with German American soldiers from other units that lasted for years after the end of the war.

It would be a mistake, however, to presume that Zoar's soldiers moved in circles pretty much like those that they left behind. To cite but one example, Zoar was staunchly Republican, and according to (apocryphal?) accounts, only one individual from the communal era is known to have voted Democrat.[68] The German Americans of the Ohio 107th were mostly Democrats—or at least so it seemed to one observer—and not all of them even supported the Emancipation Proclamation.[69] To Anthony Burkhart, who left a community with a rich patriotic and mostly pro-Lincoln heritage, it must have come as a shock to hear a Democrat fellow soldier disparage Lincoln (who was on his way to visit the troops) and claim that he would "shoot the —— Republican." Fortunately, Burkhart's comrade failed to act on this rash threat.[70]

In other words, entry into the Union army presented the soldiers from Zoar with the double challenge of dealing with new and multifaceted elements of both general American and, of a quite different kind, German American society. The esteemed elders of the Society, no matter how removed from the world of the inductees, could scarcely have remained ignorant of the social and ideological factors that would impact Zoar's young men. The Society had, in fact, been involved in humanitarian aid, as shown by a small series of letters from Canal Dover. On September 5, 1862, Louisa C. Blicksenderfer began a letter of lament about the war's impact on families and on society in general with the statement, "Once more you have surprised us with contributions to the Soldier's aid society"; in an undated note in English, Mrs. J. S. Deardorff and Mrs. Rosa Demuth gratefully wrote, "The Soldiers Aid Society of Canal Dover tender their sincere thanks to the Zoar people for their gift of a large Box of very acceptable clothing for the use of the sick and wounded soldiers of our unhappy country."[71]

Official response to the enlistment, however, came in a statement tendered September 23, 1862, as a letter of petition to David Tod, governor of Ohio. The drafters of this statement (given here in the final English version) plainly state their central dilemma: while the Principles of Separatism call for obedience to temporal authority, they also unequivocally state, "We cannot serve the state as bodily soldiers, since a Christian cannot murder his enemy, much less his friend."[72]

David Tod, Governor of Ohio[73]

The adult male members of the religious society, known by the name of Separatists of the town of Zoar, Tuscarawas County, Ohio, beg leave to represent to your consideration the following statement of facts, which they most sincerely hope and trust will receive at your hands that attention which the nature and importance of the subject in their opinions deserves.

In the year 1800, the fathers of the present members of whom the signers of this document in the german [sic] language, Jacob Silvan, Jacob Ackermann, John G. Ruof, Godfrey Lenz, Godfrey Kappel, Christian Weebel, Mathew Beeler, &c. are survivors, and now members of said society and residents of said town of Zoar, formed themselves in the town of Rothenacker, (o./a. Ehingen,) [near Ehingen] in the Kingdom of Wurttemberg into said society, and as a part and portion of their religious doctrines, held and declared it, as against their principles and consciences, but in accordance with their religious views and their understanding of the devine [sic] teachings of their Savior: "Not to kill or destroy the life of a fellow being under any circumstances whatever," but to strive and teach by precept and example, to live together in Christian-Love, Peace and Harmony.

In consequence of their views held sacred by their fathers, and now by them, living there under the despotic Government of King Fredrick the 2d of Württemberg, they suffered imprisonment, confiscation of property, and had to endure numerous other personal tortures for a period of from 12 to 16 years, until at last the king became convinced, that no change could be wrought upon their minds and resolutions, satisfied himself that they would rather suffer death, then [sic] violate the convictions of their consciences.

In the year 1817 they were banished from their homes, and as exiles they reached the shore of this Republic in that year, where freedom of thought and the privileges of worshipping their God in accordance with the dictates of their consciences were promised to them. They selected a new home in that year at the above mentioned place, where they have ever since resided, and have to the extent enjoyed those benign blessings, and are happy to state that by a life devoted to industry, economy, piety and fidelity to the civil laws of their adopted country, they have prospered commensurate with their most sanguine anticipations.

In the year 1832, by an act of the legislature of Ohio, they were incorporated as such Society.

The present unhappy and unfortunate condition of our country, however, by the late conscription act of Congress requires of them such services, which they for the reasons stated conscientiously and most earnestly have to protest against.

Fourteen young adults, not yet members, volunteered their services in the army of the U.S. [added in the German version: Because our members are unbound in every respect (in jeder Beziehung ungebunden) and—according to our Constitution—can only be asked to render voluntary but never forced services, they can take charge of their persons as they wish. Therefore, if by entering the army they have disregarded our Principles and have not fully acknowledged them, such action cannot be assumed to be normative (deßwegen ist es nicht als Richtschnur anzunehmen). The Society as a whole still maintains the same principles as in the beginning.] Twenty-eight between the ages of 18 and 45, including some not fit for service, still remain.

They therefore in conclusion again state, that the doctrines and resolutions of their fathers, as above expressed, are the doctrines and resolutions of the survivors, and descendants, of those members who are now no more.

That they are ready, prepared, and willing, in lieu of any military services, to make such a pecuniary sacrifice, as the proper authority may assess against them, and trust and pray, that through your kind attention, assistance, power and influence, the object of their wishes may be accomplished and truly relieve them from the discharge of a service, which, by the teachings of divine law and the promptings of their consciences they can and dare not perform. The signers see—German paper—hereto attached.[74]

Those who signed the German document were leaders Jacob Silvan and Jacob Ackermann, followed by more than two dozen others, including Samuel Harr (Haar), who signed for himself "and others" (how many or which other members Harr represented remains uncertain).[75] By any calculation, however, less than half of the signers would have been reasonably considered age-eligible for military service under normal circumstances. The rest were well into their forties, fifties, or even older. Most of the names of older signers appear at the top of the list; most of those of the younger signers appear near the end of the list. Is the age profile for the signers of this document a function of the fact that full members of the Society tended to be a bit older?[76] Might the age of the signers be a reflection of generational differences of opinion concerning the justification for bearing arms? Who are the unnamed "others" to whom Samuel Harr refers? Might they be other military-eligible individuals who wished to protest the bearing of arms but hesitated to be identified by name outside the Zoar community?

The German version is not addressed to the governor of the state but rather begins with the title, "Reasons Why Separatists Should Not Perform Any War Duties." This title certainly conveys the impression that the document is as much a declaration of principles as a petition for exemption from service. Was the German version intended (at least partly) as an internal statement of policy and guidelines for the Zoar community? Why was the assertion—that voluntary enlistment by nonmembers does not represent a policy shift by, or a precedent for, the Zoar Separatists—found only in the German version? Was it included in its entirety, the "German paper—hereto attached" mentioned in the petition sent to Governor Tod? Did it appear in the German version to placate those who insisted on a statement opposing any erosion of traditional standards yet omitted in the English version by those who felt that it might prejudice the governor's deliberations? Though these and other questions remain unresolved and can only be guessed at, they provide the basis for possible future inquiry.

Still another factor (deserving an entire study of its own) played a significant role in the thoughts and reactions of the Zoar community: the Society of Separatists of Zoar found itself caught in the throes of a leadership crisis in which uncertainty about just how to deal with the tragedy of the Civil War was merely one symptom. After Bäumeler's death in 1853, no individual emerged with the dynamism needed to revitalize Zoar as a communal society energized by its spiritual convictions. Initially administered well enough in its day-to-day affairs, the Society experienced no infusion of new vision or spiritual vigor. Year in and year out, venerable but evidently not very inspiring readers continued to declaim printed texts of Bäumeler's sermons in the assemblies for worship, where attendance declined even as an increasingly steady stream of the young and ambitious left Zoar.[77] Eventually the community's material fortunes foundered. The watershed years for this transition were approximately those of the Civil War.[78]

Whatever uncertainty there may have been back home about how to cope with the second major wave of enlistment by its young men in 1862, the Zoar volunteers themselves certainly did not feel personally isolated from the affection of their home community. The cash books show that on September 1, 1862, there were otherwise unspecified "expenses had on account of Volunteers" in the amount of $13.[79] Presumably these costs were for items forwarded a few days later to the Zoarite volunteers: on September 5, 1862, there is an entry for a reimbursement of $11 to John Brunny Sr. for "expenses to, at & from Cleveland Ohio on ["a visit" crossed out in MS] Errand to Militia Camp, Sept. 5/11, with Box Sundries for Volunteers."[80] It did not take one Zoar volunteer stationed in Cleveland very long at all to express his gratitude. The name of the recruit who penned the following response on the very day that the "Sundries" arrived, September 5, 1862, is unknown. Perhaps the author wrote in haste, and on behalf of his comrades, so that John Brunny Sr. could take the letter back to Zoar in person when he returned home.

Esteemed Friends!

Since we have no opportunity just now to thank you in person for your kind sharing, we wish to express, through these few lines, our most heartfelt gratitude for all the acts of friendship that you showed us earlier, and now again recently.[81] The articles that you sent us were received by all with great joy, and all consider themselves fortunate to have friends so loyal, so willing to share our lot with us, and so ready to support us.

At times last week, the rations barely sufficed to still our hunger, though now once again we have enough, even apart from what you sent us. We have good fresh bread, coffee, potatoes, beef and pork that still does not taste very good to us [Zoarites did not typically eat pork], but to which we may perhaps still need to become accustomed, as we shall probably need to face worse times, and perhaps soon. [82]

At least one non-Zoarite with a connection to the Separatists visited the community's young men at their camp. On September 24, 1862, Charles J. Woolson, of Cleveland, wrote to Christian Wiebel to report that he "went several times to see your young men who have enlisted, to ascertain that they were comfortable. At first, some of them appeared a little homesick, but afterwards they were in better spirits. I think they will do their duty, and prove themselves good soldiers."[83] A letter of uncertain authorship written from Camp Delaware, Ohio, on October 14, 1862, indicates that Woolson's assessment was indeed correct. At least based on this correspondence, it appears that the soldiers were comfortable and had adjusted well to their regimen.

Beloved Mother:

I am taking the present favorable opportunity to write you a few lines, and thereby to report to you on my present situation. I am presently healthy and hope that these few lines may likewise find you and all my friends healthy.

I heard that my friend Levi [Bimeler] has been called up, but only learned later that he can be released through payment [for a substitute], which pleases me a great deal, for it would have made me very sad if he had been forced into the military, as I feel that such would be contrary to his nature, and I hope that no more will be called up at Zoar.

Each day we have to exercise for six hours, or at least that is the order that we recently received. It would make me very happy if I could get a leave soon and could visit you, but I could scarcely pull that off; perhaps later on.[84]

While the authors of this letter and the letter from Cleveland cited above clearly missed their loved ones and appreciated tokens of support from home, neither appeared to be chafing under the duties and routines of military life. If there were any home front opposition to the war, it seems not to have expressed itself through any negative impact on the morale of Zoar's volunteers. Rather, it appears that Zoar's soldiers understood that this historically pacifist community was rallying to express continuing affection for its young men in the Union army.

From this point on, there is a fairly steady stream of correspondence from the soldiers in the field to family and friends in Zoar. Those letters receive closer scrutiny in the following chapters. Here, the question is how the Civil War was impacting the Society and its membership while some of its young men were serving under the Union colors.

The author of the letter from Camp Delaware mentioned Levi Bimeler's call for induction into the military. In the October entry of his journal, Simon Beuter reported that the draft lottery had taken place in Tuscarawas County, and two young men from Zoar, Levi Bimeler and Christian Ruof, were among those chosen. Governor Tod had taken the Society's petition for an exemption from military service into account but had not granted it outright. Those who refused induction for reasons of religion and conscience were subject to a $200 penalty.[85] Beuter praises this action of the government, refers to the Constitution of the Union as the refuge for all who are oppressed, and praises the Lord for having moved the governing powers to take this step on behalf of the fine young men who are truly the salt of the earth. On October 8 the Society paid $400 to "Drafting-Commissioner Stockwell, New Philadelphia for Levi Bimeler and Christian Ruof. Penalty, ea. $200."[86]

Meanwhile, reminders of the war continued to pour into Zoar. In addition to newspaper accounts, there was a stream of correspondence with references to the war, and not just from soldiers. Christian Zimmermann, for example, on business for the Society in Philadelphia, wrote back twice in early October 1862 to describe the impact of the war on the economy and to report what he had witnessed and learned. Philadelphia, full of soldiers, noise, and color, had taken on "a completely different appearance than before."[87] As if Zoar did not already have abundant access to the print media, he (or someone at this time) sent a newspaper clipping detailing the capture of Chambersburg on October 10, 1862.[88]

John Webb, a non-Zoarite acquaintance of David Silvan, wrote to Silvan from "Camp near Nashvile [sic]" on December 12, 1862; replete with vivid accounts of sleep deprivation, efforts to commandeer sufficient food, contacts between Union soldiers and local women in the Confederate territory, and of course the particulars of the war itself (especially in and around Chattanooga), Webb's letter leaves one wondering just why he chose to share certain details and what reaction he was expecting from Silvan.[89] From a noncontemporaneous perspective, the letter seems well-nigh perverse in certain parts.

Pauline Bimeler, of Cleveland, wrote on December 15, 1862, to her kinswoman Pauline (elsewhere Paulina) Bimeler Silvan (wife of David Silvan) in Zoar. After demurring about her command of written German, and sharing family news, the author switched to the topic of the War.

> We have had letters from John Geisler [Geissler] He was well when he wrote last and I hope that he may keep so and soon return safe home with the rest of the young men from Zoar. This war is a dreadful thing, [and] we feel it much more in the city; there is always so much talk and fuss about it here and so many of our acquaintances have been killed or wounded, to go down [the] street you can often see men with an arm or a leg cut of[f] walking around that left this city not long ago blooming in health and prosperity.[90]

The author then goes on to tell how business has suffered because of rampant inflation and a general shortage of cash.

It is about this time that the extant record includes correspondence from relatives in Germany, expressing concern about the American Civil War to family members in Zoar. L. H. Seyfang, of Eglosheim near Ludwigsburg, in a collective family letter dated December 27, 1862, to David L. Silvan (whose family name was originally Seyfang), explained that the kinsfolk in the European homeland had been following newspapers accounts of the American Civil War with alarm and regret.[91] Although not openly stated in the letter, it is possible that Seyfang and others were aware of the recent step, unprecedented among the Zoar Separatists, of young men actually volunteering for military service. Seyfang's concern may quite conceivably have been as much for the spiritual climate among the Separatists as for the temporal consequences of the war itself.

The December 1862 entries in Simon Beuter's journal took on a decidedly somber cast. By January 1863, however, the author had risen again to one of his more euphoric pinnacles of eloquence, this time in praise of the Emancipation Proclamation, declaring that "President Lincoln will stand alongside Washington as the greatest man in America's history." The entry goes on to blast "Northern traitors (Democrats)," as well as corrupt Europeans who had long considered the American republic "a thorn in the eye" and had erroneously believed that the Civil War heralded its imminent end.

Not long after this, the Society received some excellent news that surely relieved considerable pressure. On March 12, 1863, the Society's attorney, Joseph C. Hance, wrote from New Philadelphia to Jacob Ackermann to report that "the case of Goesele [elsewhere Gasely] vs. the Society has been decided by the Supreme Court at Columbus in favor of the Society."[92] The suit, involving disgruntled former Zoarites, had for years consumed enormous quantities of the Society's energies. Favorable resolution meant that at least one source of chronic concern was put to rest.

In both February and March 1863, Charles J. Woolson once more appears in the Zoar correspondence, this time to report that a worker at the sawmill had said the previous year that he could build a boat for Woolson's daughter. Woolson was unable to remember the name of the worker, who may not have said that he would but rather could do such work. Be that as it may, Woolson took the worker's statement as a promise and in his March letter applied considerable pressure to the good folks in Zoar.

> My daughter wishes me to write you and say that she hopes you have not forgotten the promise you made to build her a Boat.
>
> She says she shall be *very much disappointed* if you do not have it finished and ready for her use when she comes to Zoar, as she expects to do so on the *23rd of May!*
>
> She has *set her heart on the Boat*, and I hope you will not fail to have it ready for her.
>
> We think we shall stay 3 or 4 weeks at Zoar, and then, perhaps, we may have the boat sent up to Cleveland by Canal: or we may decide to let it remain under your care at Zoar until we come there again.[93]

One can only speculate on the reaction to Woolson's letter and to the priority that the Society's workmen may have assigned to the boat project.

Meanwhile, President Lincoln declared a Day of National Humiliation, Fasting, and Prayer on April 30, 1863. This day of commemoration provided the Society of Separatists an opportunity to reaffirm its patriotism and explain some of the positions that it took as a religious society. The following unsigned document may reasonably be associated with the papers of the Zoarite soldier Eugene B. Wright. Although Wright was at times a critic of the Society, he (or whoever wrote this text) certainly wanted to clarify the stance of the Society in the face of evident misunderstanding.

> In order to justify the behavior of the Separatists of Zoar during the present crisis, I wish to publish here a few communications. Various individuals regard them [the Separatists of Zoar] as secessionists, which is an entirely false perspective. The Separatists are unique, vastly different from all other sects. They had their beginning in the middle of the last century in Württemberg. Simply because of their noble principles, however, they had to suffer persecution and privation, which they bore willingly.
>
> Their Principles are entirely according to the teachings of the Gospel, among which is: in no instance to avenge oneself in a warlike manner or to practice the use of murderous weapons, but to suffer death rather than to murder one's fellow human or even one's greatest enemy. Hence, these their principles forbid them to go to war, even to fight for their own rights. Because their trust is placed in God, they heed God's proclamation: "Vengeance is mine, I shall repay." In this they are therefore doing what their Principles allow, something that no one can deny them in a free country. Moreover the Society, made up of Separatists, is absolutely for preservation of the Union, and the compassion for the fallen and wounded in the service of our fatherland is widespread whenever reports of such incidents are received. In order to keep abreast of such reports, one-and-a half times as many newspapers are currently received as were earlier. These are read with the greatest attention to the latest reports received by *mail and telegraph*.
>
> The Day of Penance and Prayer declared by the president [the declared Day of National Humiliation, Fasting, and Prayer] was likewise observed in Zoar—even though the Separatists otherwise

recognize no other holidays than Sunday and Christmas—with the customary practices. I wish to give here a part of the speech delivered on the appointed day.

Since Settling in Zoar, the Separatists have adhered to the rules of the Republic, and do so now more than ever, and were it not against the Principles of the Society, with respect to supporting preservation of the Union, Zoar would have a number of volunteers in the field comparable to that of other communities of the same size. However, because the Society's principles do not allow them to do so, it would be improper to disturb the Society in fulfillment of its Principles; as in other instances, the Zoar Separatists have always lived in peace with their neighbors, and indeed have as their rule the Principle of peace.

"Patriotism" is a word spoken much at this time, though perhaps it is not understood by many who call themselves patriots or is frequently misunderstood, for many a one calls himself a patriot when he enters the army as a volunteer in order, as is said, to receive good pay, good food, and good clothing, without having to do anything. If he returns, he has a good home; if he does not return, not much has been lost anyway. One can often hear this, or words to this effect, being spoken.

Now it is true that a volunteer deserves a certain respect since he puts his life entirely at stake in order to fight for his fatherland. In my view, however, this is no true patriotism if indeed one is looking more to good payment and serves his country only for good pay. Rather, a true patriot should first of all attempt to fulfill his duty as well as possible [and] only after fulfilling his duty to his own satisfaction and that of others claim his due pay, that is, if he [actually] needs it. Should he be in a position that he can make his way in life quite well, he would consider it unnecessary, in *principle,* to need to be [inducted] in order to assure being employed for the general welfare and good.[94]

There is as yet no extant indication of public reaction to Zoar's participation in the Day of National Humiliation, Fasting, and Prayer, or even of the intended audience for the text cited above. It would be especially interesting to know what discussion, if any, was provoked by the idea that a true patriot might defer or even decline compensation for services to the country.

The Society of Separatists soon learned a painful lesson in the price of patriotism. Charles J. Woolson's daughter was scheduled to arrive in Zoar

William Bimeler and his wife, Lillian Ruof Bimeler, ran the Zoar Hotel until William died in 1928. (Lillian then married Jacob Sturm.) Photo courtesy of Ohio Historical Society.

about one month later (around May 23) for a stay of some three to four weeks. If her travel plans had gone ahead as envisioned, she would have witnessed one of the community's saddest moments during the Civil War: arrival of news that Gottfried Kappel had died in Virginia.[95] This was certainly a far cry from the anticipated joy of a boat ride.

Simon Beuter's journal and William Bimeler's compilation of vital statistics and attendant notable events used identical language to describe the death of Kappel.[96] Tucked between notices that the Cider House had been completed and that the plague of seventeen-year locusts had ended is the grievous news: "Gottfried Kappel is reported to have died in the army hospital, the first to have forfeited his life in this rash undertaking [diese voreilige Unternehmung]." Neither Beuter nor Bimeler make it clear whether the phrase "this rash undertaking" refers to the war or to the enlistment of Zoarite volunteers in the armed forces.

Beuter, for his part, wrote in June 1863 that the course of the war had changed, "but not to our advantage," and that he saw Washington in greater danger than the Confederate capital. In June and July 1863 Beuter claimed to see in the inauspicious weather "the fury" and "the sorrow" of nature reacting to war. Nevertheless, he continued to record in detail the outcomes of most major battles and to show a rather keen interest in military matters than one might expect from this avowed pacifist.

For obvious reasons, those young men of Zoar who had not been drafted and had no interest in volunteering were busily seeking exemption by any means possible. David L. Silvan (born in 1839) had reluctantly become postmaster in Zoar but then used that position to request exemption. A letter from the Post Office Department in Washington, D.C., dated July 2, 1863, informed Silvan that this would not be possible: "The letter of yourself and others under date of June 25, 1863, relative to the new enrollment act has been received. The law makes no exception in favor of Postmasters, or their Assistants. They stand upon the same footing with other citizens in regard to the draft."[97] It would be interesting to know whether "yourself and others" indicates that one or more community leaders cosigned the letter of June 25, or perhaps that Silvan had made inquiry on behalf of himself and others. Since the letter clearly states that "the law makes no exception in favor of Postmasters, or their Assistants," it is possible that Silvan was attempting to obtain a declaration of exemption for himself and/or some other individual(s), such as Eugene B. Wright, a former postal assistant who had subsequently enlisted and at this period was looking for a legitimate way to leave the armed forces. It did not take long, however, for Zoar's conscientious objectors to come to terms with the reality of their situation. In a statement in English dated July 10, 1863, two dozen men stated, "We the undersigned do hereby declare that we cannot conscientiously perform militia or military duty, as required by the late militia law of the State of Ohio; but instead, we are willing to pay such fine, to which we as citizens of this state and of the United States may reasonably and equitably be subjected to."[98] Although it is not known exactly to whom these young men sent their letter, it suffices to suppose that it served as a statement of principle whenever and wherever needed. Some of the signers were from families whose members had enlisted in the Union forces: Breil, Brunny, Kappel, Kümmerle, and Rieker.[99] One, Magnus Burkhart, later entered the armed forces. This declaration may have represented to the conscientious objectors something similar to the volunteers' statement of intent to enlist: an expression of principle made publicly and without compromise.

Exactly how many times the men who signed this statement had to pay penalties is also not known, but there does exist a bundle of receipts for fines, all issued at New Philadelphia, Ohio, on September 10, 1863, and bearing the printed message "RECEIVED OF [name, of Lawrence Township] the sum of Two Dollars for Fine for nonattendance at Militia Muster during the present year, to the credit of the Military Fund."[100] All bear the signature of the treasurer (none other than Henry Andermann) and his deputy. The list of recipients of these receipts is nearly identical with that of the signers of the July 10 statement. Wrapped around the receipts is a handwritten note, in English:

> Sept. 29/63
> *Commandant*
> Of *Militia Company* of *Lawrence Township.*
> Tuscarawas County, Ohio *25 Treasurer's Receits* [sic]
> (Postmasters & Clerks of P. O. being exempt)
> Commandant will please excuse for not having
> presented within [sic] receipts at or before the
> general muster-day, if such has already taken
> place in said Township.
> Trustees, Zoar, Ohio[101]

Several seemingly unrelated items may have significance for the history of Zoar at this period, during which many of the remaining young men of the community were seeking alternatives to military training. Correspondence from September 8, 1863, and an account entry from December 1 of the same year mention transactions related to public works (in the former instance, payment for maintenance of the feeder dam to the Ohio Canal; in the latter case, construction of a culvert).[102] This all came at a period when looming military obligations lay heavy on many a young male Zoarite's mind, and it may give a clue as to the origin and date of a petition "To the Honourable The General Assembly of the State of Ohio," extant in the papers of the Western Reserve Historical Society. Undated and unsigned, the petition makes the now-formulaic references to the background and convictions of the Separatists, to their loyalty to the United States, and to the perceived unfairness of payments considered punitive for nonattendance at militia muster. The petition then concludes with the following unexpected request:

> Your Petitioners therefore pray to be exempted from performing military duty. Should there be objection to this prayer of your Petitioners

which they cannot see & which should appear insurmountable to your honourable body, your Petitioners then pray that they may at least be permitted to spend the same time, during which others attend to military training[,] in Labor on the Public Highways in lieu thereof instead of being compelled to pay a fine in money.[103]

Though there is no conclusive proof, it is not unreasonable to suggest that perhaps the drafters of this petition were hoping that current and ongoing public works projects might provide a ready-made opportunity for them to offer acceptable public service in lieu of bearing arms.

September and October 1863 brought more correspondence from Charles J. Woolson. In a letter dated September 21, 1863, he wondered whether Zoar administrators might permit him "to put an open Franklin Stove, *to burn coal*, into [the host's] large parlor" so that the Woolson daughters, "when they go down there, in a few weeks, may have a pleasant bright fire to sit by in the Evening."[104] Naturally, Woolson offered to furnish the stove at his own expense and, as in earlier asking for a boat, wrote a second letter (October 8, 1863) to reinforce his request. As a partner in the stove manufacturers Woolson, Hitchcock & Carter, this would have been a perfectly natural gesture of magnanimity on Woolson's part.[105]

The final quarter of 1863 must have been one of anxiety in Zoar. Beuter noted in his journal entries for October through December of that year that a total of some 30,000 (about two and a half times the actual number) were believed to have perished at Chattanooga. The president had called for 300,000 more troops, with 32,000 to come from Ohio, voluntarily or otherwise, by the following January 5; possible reactivation of the draft loomed large on the horizon. "As it appears, the quota for our township will be seventeen men at the next call-up"; "folks are really making strenuous efforts in our township to come up with volunteers for the next draft, and the township is paying a bounty of $200 [each] in great hopes of being able to obtain them." Financial transactions via the Society's general account by, or on behalf of, Zoar's servicemen continued apace, as indeed was the case until the war ended and the soldiers returned home. In a community that maintained extensive records of its business dealings, such use of the general account must have offered a subtle, unrelenting reminder that some one to two dozen men with ties to the Society were actively involved in the war.

Such uses of the general account were not the only transactions of note at this time. Because of the lack of earlier extant material, or perhaps

because it actually was so, one gets the impression that this was also a period of increased tempo and intensity of financial activity by the Society
in the gold markets, government and railroad bonds, and other speculative
ventures that continued beyond the end of the war.[106] During the course
of its history, the Zoar community invested in areas as diverse as dry goods
and imported hardware; its portfolios included both stocks and bonds. It
made loans to private individuals. The financial activity of this period may
reflect business acumen and/or insecurity in the face of Civil War–era
social and economic turbulence.

The Society tended to play its cards close to the chest, as it were, and
scrupulously avoided public attention to its financial dealings. Maintaining privacy was not easy, as shown by a letter dated December 12, 1863,
in English and in Christian Weebel's handwriting, to Mr. S. Hunt at Merchants Bank in Massillon, Ohio. In addition to statements relating to the
purchase of bonds, Weebel makes the following, revealing statement—the
circumstances prompting reference to attorneys and authorities are not
entirely clear, but the overall intent of the letter certainly is: "Our people,
feeling an aversion of making money-matters public; feeling an aversion
also of appearing before attorneys and county authorities—including loss
of time and expenses incurred—would consider it a lasting favor in our
government or its special authorities by exempting this establishment from
such publicity, trouble & expence [sic] in the premises, if possible."[107]

Zoar was also renowned for its charity. On November 13, 1863, the Ohio
Democrat of New Philadelphia reported that the Zoar Separatists had lent
close to $9,000 to county commissioners for relief of the families of volun-
teers.[108] This was more than twice the sum lent by the Cadiz Bank and more
than a dozen times the sum lent by one private individual, B. F. Helwig.
Such publicity no doubt prompted other parties to attempt to tap the Society's resources. In a year-end appeal dated December 28, 1863, a certain D.
Yant, of Bolivar, Ohio, wrote on behalf of the Cleveland Freedman's Aid
Commission, soliciting funds. Yant stated confidently, "I expect to be able to
raise 150 or 200 dollars in this neighborhood" and indicated that he would
"call in a week or thereabouts."[109] Yant claimed he was writing pursuant
to a recent conversation with an encouragement from "Mr. Kapple." It is
possible that "Mr. Kapple" simply discussed the Society's antislavery stand
and that Yant already knew something of the nature of the group's financial
solvency and decided that the time was right to make an appeal. Perhaps,
however, more was involved. Might the father or another relative of the

deceased Gottfried Kappel have spoken with Mr. Yant because he desired a way to commemorate the deceased soldier's sacrifice through a benevolent contribution, or something of the sort?

The year 1864 did not start on a more auspicious note than that on which the outgoing year ended. Simon Beuter's January entry included mention of harsh cold, much snow, and winds that claimed the lives of many soldiers and left others crippled for life. In February he recorded the passing of Gottfried Lenz, the last Separatist spiritual "warrior" to have suffered physically (albeit no doubt pacifistically) for his faith in the European homeland. On March 3, by order of the trustees, the Society paid the Volunteer Bounty Fund of Lawrence Township $400 for Levi Bimeler and Christian Ruof.[110] And, for the first and only time, a Civil War–related death took place in Zoar itself—Eugene B. Wright deserted and returned home to die of tuberculosis on March 29, 1864, at just under twenty-two years of age.

In April 1864 Christian Zimmermann again visited Philadelphia and once more wrote back a series of letters to the Society with information on economic conditions.[111] While Zimmermann reported less on the details and progress of the war than in previous letters, it is clear that he attributed acute and rapid inflation to the war. Within the space of just one week, he had seen some prices rise dramatically. It was generally believed, he reported, that market conditions would deteriorate before they improved.

Market conditions were only part of the Society's concerns, of course. In his May 1864 journal entries, Simon Beuter stated that on three occasions the Society was able to purchase its young men freedom from the draft and had paid bounty money on behalf of Levi Bimeler and Christian Ruof. "Our Society has, up to this point, lost those who went as volunteers." Did Beuter mean that the Society had lost the loyalty of the volunteers to the Principles of Separatism, or merely that it had lost the opportunity to purchase these men's exemption from military duty? If he meant the former, the trend toward decline in Society membership was already set in motion, with or without the events of the Civil War. If Beuter meant the latter, it is doubtful that those who had enlisted as volunteers, with one possible exception to be discussed later, would have been interested in having the Society pay an exemption fee on their behalf.

It is ironic that only a few lines above this statement concerning the "loss" of the Zoar volunteers, Beuter recorded the outcome of the Battle of Richmond, and that with obvious interest in the victory of the Union forces. If there is one trend that is consistent in Beuter's journal for the

Civil War years, it is this: he did not want to fight the war but delighted in cheering for his favored side in the conflict.

For all that, Beuter was no optimist, though a not-altogether sanguine outlook is understandable in view of the times in which he wrote the journal entries. In the margin of his journal, Beuter routinely indicated and summarized the subject of the entry in the main text that it accompanied. In July 1864 his marginal note reads "[my] own feelings"; the statement in the actual journal entry included the frank admission that "especially apprehensive feelings are stalking me." No wonder: on that same page, Beuter explains that the president had just called up another 500,000 men, with the quota to be met by volunteer enrollment or whatever other means necessary.

By the end of August those who wished to pay for a substitute learned a hard lesson in supply and demand. A letter from Simon Beuter dated August 29, 1864, vividly reflects the difficulty that the Society faced. Beuter, in Cincinnati, stood poised to pay substitutes at the market price and wished authorization to move in a decisive manner.

Esteemed Friend,

I am herewith letting you know how the prospects are for volunteers here. Today we worked as much as we could from morning until now; the success was not altogether bad, we have enlisted two men, and have the pledge of nine men until tomorrow at 9:00, but the price is high: we cannot get them for less than the $450 reported yesterday, and the costs for Haly and Stout, though I just saw a man who demanded the same amount and no more. If he can do something, we can get through the matter that much quicker. If we do not offer the above sum, there are others who are glad to pay it, and I am even more afraid because people are still coming who are looking for recruits. The city is almost full.

Now you [plural] should write to us right away whether we should proceed or not; naturally, it will cost our Society some of the $1,000 that was last promised; at first I thought we could get by without using it, but at the above-mentioned price that won't be the case.[112] But if I could advise, I would not consider the matter of money, since the people at home have absolutely no idea what a soldier's life is like. Just in the camps, those who have just come from their homes are almost all sick since they get nothing but hard crackers and stinking bacon.

And, if our people would actually come into the hospitals, Zoar would be a paradise by comparison. Folks who have lived so long in Zoar don't have any notion what a desolate world it is, despite the small passing inconveniences [in Zoar]. [113]

The Society's understanding of a soldier's life appears to have undergone considerable reconsideration since the Day of National Humiliation, Fasting, and Prayer some sixteen months earlier.

A penciled note on the envelope containing the above text indicates agreement to allocate the market price of $450, presumably for as many paid substitutes as may be needed.

In his September journal entries, Beuter was as astounded as he was relieved that the 500,000 men demanded by the president had been recruited in great part through voluntary enlistment. The next time around, the Society wanted to take no chances and on January 25, 1865, prepaid $1,200 to the "volunteer fund of Lawrence Township . . . preparatory for the coming draft." [114] One might say that the Society had chosen to take preemptive action.

In April 1865 Beuter reported the assassination of Lincoln in pathos-laden language and the surrender of Lee in the ebullient tone that marked his more festive journal entries. He exercised his best didactic style in July to report the execution of President Lincoln's assassins. And in December of that year, in his year-end summary, Beuter reported rather laconically that most of the Zoarite soldiers had returned.

The next year, on June 29, 1866, Marie Seyfang wrote from Eglosheim, Germany, to David Silvan. [115] In the letter, she rejoices that the American Civil War has ended and expresses her own horrified impressions of what must have happened during the course of that conflict.

In 1867 the Society—or some individual(s)—paid one dollar each for five lifetime patrons' memberships in the U. S. Soldiers' Orphans Home in Columbus, Ohio. [116] With the receipts for this donation, the documentation for the involvement of the Society of Separatists in the Civil War comes to a close; the following chapters turn to the accounts of individual soldiers.

Eugene B. Wright

Perspectives of the Individual and of the Society

The largest body of Civil War–related material from Zoar documents the experiences of Eugene B. Wright.[1] In the account of his early life there, Wright offers invaluable insights into day-to-day life at Zoar during the period of his childhood. The recipient of special schooling, Wright may have been groomed at one point for leadership in the Society.

We have nothing parallel to this autobiographical statement as background information for any of the other Zoarite soldiers. The part cited here is from 1860.

I was born in [MS blank] on June 26, 1842. Because of special circumstances, my parents brought me here, to Zoar, when I was only half a year old.[2] This is where I have been since. I was received and raised here in a friendly way by the Society, as though I were one of their own. I was instructed along with their own children, and even more so. I and a comrade of mine, Johannes [John] Geissler, and later also David Silvan, had, in addition to the usual school, two hours of instruction in the evening from my good friend J. M. Bäumler [Bimeler], preacher and leader of the community. I was raised under the friendly supervision of [the elder] David Silvan, who was not lacking in friendly admonitions that, as in the case of most children, I did not properly heed, which I now regret. He, however, died February 29, 1854, at 10:00 A.M., at the age of 58 years.[3] I was left, up to the present time as I write this, under the supervision of his spouse, Jakobina Silvan. She also was not lacking in well-intentioned admonitions that in part still remain unheeded.

When I became old and strong enough to do light work, I had to help the above-mentioned David Silvan with trees and such. He was an orchard- and nurseryman. When I reached my 14th year, I also wanted to learn a trade. Up until that time I had to work in the field, and since I had no chance to learn the merchant's trade, I came here to the print shop, where I received some instruction from Christian Zimmermann and Matthäus Mack. . . . [However,] I could not get ahead alone and so worked again a bit longer than one year, usually at fieldwork, until the year 1858.

I then came once again to the print shop, to a certain Heinrich Hiessrich, who was from Pittsburgh, Pennsylvania, and a trained typesetter. I worked with him for about a year. Then—because of his unseemly conduct—he had to leave.[4] For a period I had to carry on the business alone, until in the year 1859, when a comrade of mine, Ludwig Heid, came to help me. For a period in 1859, I also needed to help out in the Zoar Store.

At this time I made all kinds of experiences and learned how, with sufficient diligence, I should develop my understanding . . . but would sometimes forget myself again and fall back into my old ways. As I look at my conduct of life, I was not one of the most virtuous. I was a light-hearted and proud lad and often had a mind to do better, but it did not last long. Still, by the grace of God, I was always held in check so that until now I have not been the worst, and I hope also that he will further deign to take me under his protection and help me to attain a better walk of life.

In religious matters in general I did not wish to be narrow-minded but was always held in that state, for on Sundays I had to attend service three times and in the winter read the Bible for an hour prior to the after-school instruction, whereas others could go to church when they wished. I would sometimes make a sour face, but I could not do otherwise, and needed to conform even though it was hard enough on me. I thought: if it were possible to lead a proper life, it would not matter so much if one sometimes had a little enjoyment on Sundays or otherwise. But so far I have survived and will be able to do so until I have reached my adulthood.

Concerning my staying here . . . I thought one could lead just as good and pious a life somewhere else as here in Zoar. Almost daily I saw that those who were members of the Society did not distinguish themselves from others in matters of virtue but rather did just the opposite. Hence I felt it had not been proven that God could only find pleasure in a person who stayed here yet might otherwise do as he wished. For this reason I never said for certain, nor do I say now, that I shall stay here. For still other reasons, I have no desire to stay.[5]

In 1860 I was allowed to visit my father in Wooster, Ohio. At that time it was virtually up to me whether I wanted to come back here or not. I went but at the end of one week returned and decided, should nothing special occur, that I would stay here until I reached my adulthood.

In the meanwhile, various things took place that ran contrary to my will, such that I knew that I owed the Society at Zoar a great deal for my friendly upbringing, and that I would do a great favor by my extended stay here and by completion of my work, namely, publishing a book of sermons by J. M. Bäumeler. And so I decided to complete it but at the same time to assume no other function in Zoar than that of a merchant. Through the next summer I worked at my task until the harvest, when I helped out for about three weeks and then returned to my job.

One main reason why I was not willing to stay here was the narrow-mindedness in religious and political matters. For the Separatists abstained from everything in politics except voting. No one was allowed to attend a public meeting, be it on whatever topic, nor any exhibition, and above all not any entertainment, a prohibition that I transgressed on September 31, 1860, when two comrades and I went to Canal Dover, Ohio, and attended a county fair, for which I was scolded. Still, I did not much worry about it but rather have decided to go again at the next opportunity. It was also not permitted to go to any place outside Zoar on Sundays, which I also sometimes did.

Sometimes I went to a neighbor['s,] where we spent time singing and playing music with one of the daughters. For that I was soundly reproached but did not worry about it, for I could find nothing wrong with it and hence did as I pleased. Hence there was also much gossip about me, for the people in Zoar believed that I did all sorts of bad things when I went there or had too much social contact with those girls. Most of the gossip arose from envy that some of the women felt toward me. I did not turn back, however, but rather believed and did as I wished in this regard.

What might these Zoarites be rehearsing? Haydn's *Die Schöpfung* (*The Creation*)
was a favorite work among the Zoarites. Zoar also maintained an active band
from around 1840 until the Society's dissolution in 1898. Photo courtesy of Ohio
Historical Society.

In autumn of the year 1860, I started to learn to play the piano
and one of my comrades and I began a small music band. I found a
joy in music but until then had not gone far with it. I soon gave both
up again, namely, the piano music and the music band, because of
the deportment of one of my comrades who had progressed quite
a bit through much effort. He so instructed us that it displeased me;
I gave up both and spent my extra time with drawing and such. I
enjoyed this very much though I had no teacher, but rather simply
learned it by myself. . . . I also often had impulses to write down my
views about certain things, but I could not get to it until now. I am
writing this at the end of 1860. Something always came in the way
whenever I wanted to get to this.

In November 1860 we began operating our new print shop in a
new building near the Store. Until then, our print shop had been

on the second floor of the Store. I now had a better opportunity to follow my inclination. The former Store used to close each night at 8:00 P.M. Then we had to get out as well. This was the appointed time for work in the store, even throughout the winter. Hence I did not have much opportunity while working in the Store to do something for myself of this sort [e.g., writing an autobiography]. In our new office, I could virtually stay as long as I wished, except for the fact that the old woman who raised me, and with whom I still lived, did not want me to come home so late, regardless where I'd been. She would become discontent, and therefore I often returned home earlier in order not to offend her.

I had an inner respect for all people, but I preferred a room of my own so that I could be undisturbed in the pursuit of my goal and generally in order to feel freer in all things. I could not conform to the order and rules of these folks, though I wished with God's help to be able to lead a virtuous, righteous life so that in my youth I might lay the foundation for my future happiness. Therefore I also denied the acquaintance of my beloved [left blank] and decided, supported by the well-meaning advice of my father, to avoid all such acquaintance at least until I had attained adulthood, or—as I did not intend to stay at Zoar—until I had learned more about the general ways of the world. With the beginning of the year 1861, I decided to change my life, and especially to pass my leisure time in a useful, or at least not in a bad way, as did so many of the friends of my youth. I hope to be able to observe this rule for the length of my life, with the help of God, who is the protector of all that is good, and who thus far has so received me and, as I hope, will also never leave me.[6]

In a statement from Zoar dated January 23, 1861, Wright laid out in English the following principles. Although his intended readership remains uncertain, what is clear is that Wright was overflowing with idealistic enthusiasm. If he indeed believed what he wrote—and there is no reason to assume he did not—this young man was ripe for possible disillusionment in an imperfect world and potentially an easy target for the abusive.

Try to be a useful member of mankind, and be faithful and true to my duty. Not to join bad companies, like drinking parties or like that or to spend my money for useless things, and especially for drinks, as it is the commencement of a mischievous life, as swearing, lieing [*sic*], stealing, and all vice of that kind, which only can have bad effects on future life [crossed out in MS: a happy life]. To respect old virtuous people, as young people also do wish [some day] to grow old. To join divine devotions, but not to be limited or confined and only to join freely, when I feel it necessary or useful, as I can't see any good effects from confined worshipping, as it is only by form, and is not the cause or matter of the heart, and therefore cannot better anybody.

In the present political crisis, if necessary, I would join my country-men and fellow-citizens to serve for my beloved country and liberty, as liberty is a great blessing of our God; happy must anybody, or a whole nation, be in the enjoyment of that blessing (bestowed to the American nation by kind Providence), if only it would not be misused!

To spend my leisure hours with something useful, and not to run around and do mischieve [*sic*], as so many young folks do; I am not against looking for a girl, but would like to have a virtuous, faithful and industrious, and no proud one, and to be obedient to her parents, and faithful to her acquaintances; and if she stays at home, and does not visit any dance or such company like them, I am not fond of them; I believe they don't bring any good effects on young folks, and especially ladies or girls, I believe it would be much better for them to stay at home, and do some work, or if that would not be necessary, to amuse themselves on books or something like that.

To keep the truth in all cases; and not cheat anybody only to take the part which I can call my own, with right; not to use bad or ugly words, and not to swear at no condition.

If I ever should come into bad affairs of any kind I will always trust on our God, and think that he, who protects and watches so many, will also take me in his protection, and will keep me off the path of sin, and to keep me in the hour of temptation; and hope that He will give me power to follow these things as long as He shall tell me to enjoy life, and I may progress in Virtues, as that is the only way to true happiness.[7]

The pensive and sensitive Wright could also be a fun-loving and jolly chap. Consider the following undated item signed by Eugene B. Wright and Lewis Haid (Ludwig Heid). If the Wednesday evening mentioned here was the evening before July 4, this statement dates from the summer of 1861.

The Zoar fire brigade with its wagon, behind the Zoar Hotel, ca. 1869. Photo courtesy of Ohio Historical Society.

Esteemed Fellow-Citizens,

Since we have reached a fair consensus to bring out the old fire pump, I have taken the liberty to make Lewis' and my opinion known. As July 4th is rushing upon us, I thought it most appropriate if, after dinner on the 4th, we would come out and march around in our city, with a first-class band at the front consisting of about six musicians with old instruments so that there would not be much lost if one were to be broken. One or two with axes and two with the fire hook and a small ladder of two rungs would follow the musicians. Next comes the team with the pump, and finally, the hose cart. The musicians should all have caps on, and the captain should be especially decked out with a cap and a coat and a white sash tied around him, on his right side the megaphone and on the left a staff will be attached, for the captain needs to be given detailed obedience. This is my opinion, decide for yourselves, and if you are willing to do this, let us get everything ready by Wednesday after supper.[8]

Your fellow-citizens

In a document dated January 1862, Wright once again made a detailed statement of his principles on certain issues. In English, this document includes an appended attempt to explain the sounds represented by the German alphabet and to give an approximate pronunciation of the numbers one through ten in German. There are handwritten corrections, indicating that perhaps this was a draft copy kept by Wright when he sent off the final copy. Though little is said that is new, there is a significantly different tone here: the statement of principles from January 1861 might well have been shared with anyone who wished to know Wright's feelings on certain issues; the intended reader of this statement is evidently an individual in whom the author wishes to vest an uncommon measure of private confidence. Did Wright send this to a member of his original family? Did he intend these words for some personal confidant outside Zoar, or perhaps even for the eyes of a young woman whom he had met and admired?

> I take the present as a favorable opportunity, to make You somewhat acquainted with my present principles and rule, for I think it partly necessary, to inform You about [them]. I wish You will think about, and will please and inform me, of your true opinion about [all this]. In the first place do I avoid all such societies, as: Balls, Dances &c. or in general all parties, that may effect an excessive or vicious life, which has frequently been the case; to attend to a respectable life, and especially to practice and use a moral expression. I do intend never to join any religious society, as it mostly soon becomes only a custom, or fashion, but to serve my Lord only when I feel the necessity of it, always to act according to truth, as truth is very necessary to show a virtuous and respectable life; always to respect old folks; and to void [sic] all useless expenses of money, as it often causes disadvantageous consequences; to devote my leisure hours or times to a useful or at least no bad use of time; in general, to practice a respectable and virtuous life, with the help of my Saviour, who has always taken so much care of me.
>
> These are the principle rules I intend to follow, and I wish You would not show these lines to any, and will not disappoint my confidentness [sic].
>
> I shall feel very happy to know, that You would assist me in doing good, so that we both may enjoy a really happy life, which only can be attained by virtue. Let us try to follow virtue in all cases, that we

may please our kind God, who has been with us, since we are living, and who has given us so many chances to enjoy ourselves. Happy shall we follow a virtuous life, He will not forget us, if we pray to Him, and put our whole confidence unto Him; I know He will listen to our prayers, if they are honest; I have examples of this; let us always be thankful for His great goodness bestowed to us.

I hope the contents of these lines will not be disagreeable to You; they are the true sentiments of Your best friend, who wishes to see you really happy, and who wishes Your true and honest opinion about this. May God be with us, and strengthen us in the hours of temptation, and may He in future time take care of us both is the wish of Yours [unsigned].[9]

The second part of Wright's autobiography begins in a script and on paper that are slightly different. The tone makes clear, however, that this is a conscious continuation of the author's preceding autobiographical narrative.

In the year 1862, in the middle of January, we finished our printing work, having completed the third volume of the *Versammlungsreden* [the so-called *Discourses*] of Bäumeler, and we had no desire to begin another.[10] My helper L[udwig] H[eid] entered the millwright shop, and I did this and that until a favorable opportunity presented itself to me to go into the merchant business. In the meantime, I also learned how to make brooms but attained no skill in that. In February I once again took up the merchant's trade in the Store here, and in March went to the Zoar Station that had been sold by the Society to Karl Ehlers' helper. This continued until harvest, when I returned to Zoar and worked in the harvest since there was not much to do at the Station.[11]

The remainder of Wright's autobiography, dealing with induction into the military service of the Union, is given in the preceding chapter. Before he joined the Union forces, however, Wright must have spoken with his biological parents about the prospect of service as a soldier. Unfortunately, the following (draft?) letter in English does not bear a date. It does reveal that Wright expected to be exempt from duty because of his position as a postal assistant. At the same time, he yearned to express actively his patriotism, if necessary in the military service. Similarly mixed feelings about how best to serve his country haunted Wright for the rest of his short life.

Dear Parents,

I feel myself indebted to You, for not writing sooner; I would have wrote sooner, but as harvest time came on, I neglected to write, but as I am now at my old trade again I have [a] better chance to write; I wish Your kind excuse. I wish these lines will find You in the same state of good health and happiness like I am enjoying by writing this. My health has, since my last letter, been very good, wish Yours had [been the] same; also the general health of our place has been tolerably good.

We cannot complain about our crops, for our wheat is middling good, and all other kinds of fruit are doing well, Wheat, Rye and Oats we have hauled in, nearly, and Corn & Potatoes are seeming to become excellent, since we have had some good rains; had we not received rain for the last weeks, Corn & Potatoes would have been very scarce, but now, if nothing else happens, we are waiting for an excellent crop of Corn & Potatoes.

In your last letter you state, that I should not go to War, for not being experienced for it, that's so, and I believe I would not be compelled to go, as I am incorporated to the Post Clerks in our Postoffice [sic] which are (to general Post O. rule) exempt from militia duties, but yet I feel it a part of my duties to do something for my country, if necessary if it shall be my destination of Providence, I believe I may have [a] chance for it.[12]

Another undated (draft?) letter in English, to an undisclosed recipient, reflects the admiration that Wright held for those who had chosen the path of active military service. Might this have been written to one of Zoar's earlier volunteers, or perhaps to an outsider whom Wright had met?

Dear Friend!

I feel happy to have a chance to write some lines to You, which I hope will find You in the enjoyment of best health and happiness, which will be the greatest blessing for You, to perform your hard, but patriotic and self-sacrificing duty, to which performance I hope our almighty God may strengthen You to fulfill a holy duty, and may keep You, to join the happiness of Your parents, brothers & sisters, and all Your good friends, which are anxious to have you in their circle again, as a *true Defender of our beloved Country*.[13]

Under the text of this letter, the word "Defender" is twice written in a somewhat more carefully executed script. Does this word express what Wright himself really wanted most to become?

Eugene B. Wright did enlist in the Union army, though as a soldier he did not fare well. Inducted in the late summer of 1862, he was suffering health problems by midautumn of the same year. Immediately after relating the events of his entry into the armed forces, cited earlier, Wright reported the following—it is the last entry in his autobiography, though not his last autobiographical statement.

I, however, received a leave because I was suffering from diphtheria and rheumatism. The leave was set at eight days, though according to the attestation of the Regiment physician (Charles A. Hartman), I had not yet recovered by the end of the leave. Hence, with a doctor's certificate, it was possible to extend the leave to four weeks. Only after five weeks did I return to the Regiment that, by then, was in Virginia. I left my home on November 24, 1862, and went by railroad to Washington D.C., where I arrived between 6:00 and 7:00 P.M. I stayed overnight at the so-called Soldiers' Home, where I also received board.[14]

Copies of two unsigned letters appear to deal with Wright's medical leave. All circumstances point to Wright as the author. The first is dated Camp Delaware, October 16, 1862.

I am taking the liberty of directing my lines to you and therein laying forth my wish, namely, to request a leave from you until I am again capable of serving. For I believe my illness could be healed sooner if I were at home, since I would not be exposed to all the various harsh weather such as we have here. In my present condition I cannot be of use to my fatherland, but much rather a hindrance, if I need to be fed and clothed by the government when I cannot render any service in return.

Perhaps it is possible that I shall never again be capable of service, since even before I entered the life of a soldier, I had a completely different occupation from the present one, one in which I was not exposed to the harsh weather as I am now. Because I was already afflicted at that time by joint pains and neck aches, it might easily be possible that, in my present state, I could never again become capable of service. Already upon entering the ranks of a soldier, I thought that I would not be able to endure for long but considered it only my duty to go. I have now seen that I am more of a liability to my fatherland than an asset by being fed, clothed, and paid when I can render no service in return. On this account, I thought to ask you for a leave, since then I could at least take better care of myself and perhaps sooner become once more capable of fulfilling my duties.[15]

The second is a draft and final version of a letter whose circumstances likewise indicate that Wright was the author. The only significant difference between the draft and the final version is the omission in the following final version of the mention of a certain Dr. Black.

Zoar, Tuscarawas County, October 30, 1862
Captain Richard Feederle!
    I received your letter of the 26th of the month this morning and note among other things that I am supposed to return to the Regiment under all circumstances.
    If I were capable of fulfilling my duties, I would have returned without a second thought. I have not done so only because my situation has not improved, and because Dr. Hartman reported that, if after eight days I were incapable of performing my duties, the physician who is treating me [and continuing to do so?] should send a certificate to him, Dr. Hartman, until I am once more capable of serving, at which time I must find the regiment. This is exactly what I have done, and shall continue to do, until I am capable of serving.
    It seems somewhat inexplicable to me that Col. Meyer would make accusations to you that I had overextended my leave, since he himself signed the order of leave and Starkweather issued it. Dr. Hartman, in fact, advised me how the neck pain might be alleviated most quickly, but that I would only be ready to serve if I had no neck pain, and not before. Since I still have rheumatic pain, and for military exercises must walk as much and as quickly as is necessary, I

wish to be excused until I am able to serve, and remain with respect,
[three blank horizontal lines].[16]

Others took an interest in Wright's case. Heinrich Andermann, of
New Philadelphia, who offered advice to the Zoar community on matters financial and legal and on occasion purchased Zoar cheese to take to
soldiers in camp, offered his services in a letter dated November 17, 1862:
"I am also enclosing a letter with [other] enclosures for Eugene B. Wright.
Be so kind and see to it that he gets it as soon as possible, so that he can
be ready for his trip [back to camp]. It appears to me that he has no other
choice but to show up. If he finds that he is not sufficiently recovered to
carry out his duty, I hope they will grant him his discharge. You will see
to it that he obtains a proper certification of his illness from the doctors."[17]
The Society did appeal on Wright's behalf, but not until much later.

In the meanwhile, Wright did indeed return, and his initial correspondence sets a rather positive tone. It was written to David Silvan from near
Fairfax Courthouse, Virginia, on November 29, 1862.

Friend David!

I am using the present favorable opportunity to write to you and
report how it is going just now. Yesterday at 4:00 P.M., we left Camp
Convalescent, located about one mile west of Alexandria. We then
marched slowly to the camp located about 14 miles away, where our
regiment is stationed near Fairfax Courthouse, arriving all tired out
at 10:00 P.M.

I soon found my comrades, who are all healthy, safe, and sound as
ever. It appears that Leo [Kern] enjoyed good times in the hospital,
because when he came out, he weighed 166 lbs., which doesn't indicate any great loss.

The Heiker Regiment is attached to the 107th Regiment, and
Heiker appears to be a capable officer.

The Box is not yet here, but we have apprised the quartermaster
so that he will deliver it to us. . . .

General Siegel also visited this regiment and told the officers and
soldiers how they should act and that right and justice should prevail,
which in any case would be of paramount importance in such a situation.[18]

Less than a week later, on December 1, 1862, Wright was demoted in rank from sergeant to private, at which rank he remained for the duration of his service. To what extent issues of health or still other concerns played a role in shaping his subsequent attitude toward serving in the armed forces remains a matter of conjecture. What is certain is that Wright soon began to express an objection, based on conscience and spiritual principles, to participation in the war. Wright's own attitude toward the military may quite conceivably have played a role in the decision to reduce him in rank from sergeant to private.

In a letter from Zoar dated January 20, 1863, the elders of Zoar expressed their inability to intervene on behalf of Wright, who evidently had recently stated a desire to remove himself from the armed forces.

Esteemed Friend Eugene B. Wright, we received your letter of the 3rd of this month on the 12th. It may seem a bit strange that we hesitated so long to send back a response to your request. The reasons for this lie with us. First of all, when we learned of your decision, we decided to report this to your father in person and to learn his view on the matter. On the appointed day when Georg Ruof set out to do this, he was hindered by unfavorable weather and needed to postpone the visit for several days.

As we now see from your letter, you have no prospect of being freed or released from military service because of Biblical scruples and have found yourself moved by a certain inner drive to decline all military service as entirely against true spirituality, the teachings of our Lord and Master, and against the Principles of Separatism We also wish from our hearts that these principles may be impressed ever more firmly, and with ever more conviction, upon your heart and spirit. For God is always ready to maintain a person outside the condition into which all of us have put ourselves through our own will, if the individual is serious about this and has this as his firm purpose, for without a struggle, no one can prevail as victor.

Now, concerning the possibility mentioned in your letter of obtaining a substitute for you, and that that might be easier achieved here, such is not the case. We would never be able to come to peace with ourselves for going against our conscience. Also, you can no doubt judge, or might know, into what a position we put the Trustees in such a case, and that we cannot lightly do such a thing without subjecting ourselves to sure reproach, or without arousing dissatisfaction if we were to pay a certain sum of money on your behalf.

Indeed, there are parents of some of our enlisted young people who have not yet felt or expressed any inclination such as you have toward serving in the military. Moreover, we have been informed by persons who know for certain that it is very difficult, if not impossible, to find a man who would voluntarily enlist in the place of another.

Now if it is your firm decision and serious intention to follow through as you feel within yourself, then we desire and pray to God with all our heart that He might let his grace abound toward you and give you strength and courage to bear with all patience whatever you may need to suffer and endure. We certainly know that God is compassionate and merciful and will not lay upon a person more than one is in a state to bear.

In may seem unexpectedly harsh to receive such news, but that is all we can do at this time and under the present circumstances. We commend you to the special protection of God and his grace, that he may soon again lead you back into our midst, safe and sound.

Let us know again how you are and how it is going for the others. Thank God, we are all healthy and doing well so far. We greet you and also your comrades; also, a greeting from your foster mother Jakobina; we remain herewith your friends,

Jakob Ackermann[,] John G. Ruof[, and] Samuel Haar [Harr][19]

This letter is interesting on several counts. Already, in 1861, the Society had hoped that payment for substitutes would allow conscientious objectors to avoid induction into military service altogether. Wright's voluntary enlistment, however, had placed him into quite a different category. Moreover, although the Society was opposed to war, it seems that the parents of those who had enlisted were not stating any open objection to their sons' participation. Indeed, the Zoarites were unflinchingly in favor of the Union and may have been loathe to do anything that would seem to disparage the support to this cause given by their young men who did choose to enlist. As the authors of the letter openly admit, Wright's case left the trustees of the Society in an awkward position, both publicly and privately.

There may also have been a wait-and-see attitude concerning Wright himself. On February 19, 1863, Jacob Ackermann wrote the first of a series of letters in which one or more senior members of the Zoarite community suggested that Wright might free himself from his obligation to military service through proper application of "situational ethics."

Dear Friend Eugene!

We are happy to have learned from your last letter written to David that you have no reason to complain about your health, though we were concerned that there still does not appear to be any happy news forthcoming to indicate that you could be released from the military status that strives against the teaching of our Savior Jesus Christ, as you yourself have come to recognize from your own convictions. We also ask God that he would maintain and strengthen this conviction in your heart, for God never lays upon the individual more than that person is in a condition to bear, if such is accepted in patience.

We recently learned from a letter that Christian Rieker wrote to his brother that he was of the opinion that, with time, you could be back home again if you accepted the offer made to you by your superiors, namely if you accepted an assignment [i.e., commission] and served for a period of time, and then resigned it and returned home. If that were so, it is our opinion that you would not go very far wrong by doing so. You can better find out about that there than we can here at home. Or one might do as many appear to have done, who have allowed themselves to be drummed out. For many, this is impossible to do, but what all will one *not* do in order to be released from a condition that is contrary to his inner conviction!

It filled us with regret when we recently learned that Miller is supposed to have declared that there is no other alternative [for the soldier who declines to serve as commanded] to being placed under punishment, whether for three years or for the duration of the war. May God forbid that in your case, as we fear that you might not be rugged enough to endure it, though with God nothing is impossible if the will of the person is a serious intent to live according to God's will and to serve him. Our wish and prayer is that he would receive you and keep you in his fatherly protection.

For our part, we are rather well and all goes on as usual, apart from the fact that we feel very much the great loss that we have experienced because so many of our young people have suddenly left. We greet you and your comrades and remain your friends![20]

Jakob Ackermann served as a trustee of the Society of Separatists of Zoar from 1832 until his death in 1889. This photograph was taken ca. 1880–89. Photo courtesy of Ohio Historical Society.

Meanwhile, in three letters written by Wright to David Silvan from near Brooks Station, Virginia, the author expresses no particular discontent with military life. Indeed, he seems more occupied with the sale of a watch to John Geissler, and with maintaining the network of contact with other Zoarite soldiers, such as John Geissler and Johannes Kücherer. The first of these letters, dated February 23, 1863, strikes a rather positive tone.

Dear Friend David!
Since John Geissler let me know via Kücherer that he wishes I would send home money to him and address it to you, I am using the present opportunity to fulfill his wish. I am transmitting to you $10.00 in the hope that it will arrive at its proper destination. In fact, Geissler wanted me to send it express, but as there is no chance to do that here, I decided to send it on via the mail, and I believe it is as secure as if sent express. If you receive it, please let me know as soon as possible.

I still have $5.15 of his money on hand that I am maintaining for the following reason. I promised Geissler my watch, and he wrote me that I should hold onto the value [of the watch]. I recently received a letter from him, as he is still in Aquia Creek in the hospital. But, as J. Kücherer reported, he has since been sent to Washington, whence he will write to you. You could also send him my address since we don't know in which hospital he is and thus cannot write to him. I hope he would have the luck of being discharged in the hospital, but the Almighty will also lead his destiny to the best [outcome], and may [He] also liberate me through his almighty hand.

The wish of [myself,] your friend[,] is that the Almighty may protect you and also us. We greet you, Paulina and her mother, as well as your sister Wilhelmina, [and] your and my friend Samuel (from whom I have wished to receive an answer for some time now); also greet Wiebel, Barbara, Christian and Ludwig, and Petermann's and August's families, and as a cordial closing, especially old motherly Jakobina. Along with a friendly greeting from a distant friend, I remain, while awaiting an answer.[21]

A second letter dated March 1, 1863, begins in a rather homespun and cheerful manner.

Dear Friend David!
    While you are perhaps assembled at this hour in quiet Zoar, singing praise to God, the kind giver of all that is good, I have set myself down alone on the hill located near our camp in order to write a brief letter in response to [you,] my friend, including all your loved ones, though I know nothing particular about which to write.[22]

Wright then goes on to discuss the details of the pocket watch sale and to ask about the best way to send mail to John Geissler. The third letter of March 3, 1863, makes no statements of gross dissatisfaction on the part of the author.

Dear David,
    I'll use this favorable opportunity [provided] by [commanding officer] Müller. I wish you would write me and send envelopes and, if possible, some stamps. Of course, I would prefer to come myself, but presently that is impossible—as you well know.

It would also please me if you [plural] would send me one of the small songbooks printed at Zoar and, if possible, some of the Sunday meditations [Versammlungsreden].

Greet all [my] friends and write to me again soon.

Most cordially,

Eugene

[P.S.] It just occurred to me that I could use a scissors, as one of the other [soldiers] lost mine.[23]

Nevertheless, Wright must have been expressing some form of strong discontent with army life. Jakob Ackermann, in response to a letter by Wright of March 1, 1863 (not in the extant record), became even more blatant in his appeal to Wright to avail himself of any and every opportunity to leave the military, implying that the end would justify the means. The following letter, dated March 13, 1863, suggests just how difficult it must have been for all parties to deal patiently with this situation.

Esteemed Friend Eugene B. Wright!

We have duly received your letter of the 1st of this month and see from it that, except for one individual, you and your comrades are fairly healthy, though in your own case there appears to be no favorable change concerning your release from military service. We see from your letter that various positions have been offered to you in which you would at least not need to bear arms, and thereby be free of the military standing that you find so burdensome.

That you have made a firm decision to have nothing to do with the support or aid of the war is well and good, insofar as such strives against Christ's teachings. That you hesitate to accept such a position in order finally to go free, fearing that doing this in effect attempts to deceive your fellow man and hence runs counter to the calling of a Christian and indeed of every person of character, is something that we view differently.

We believe in this matter that war is no righteous matter anyway, nor can it be, and that one may seize the chance to be released without deception or causing harm. Many others take advantage of such an opportunity in order to be free of the repulsive state of serving as a soldier.

All in all, we leave it entirely to your conviction and perspective to do as you wish and can in this matter. We advise you to ponder in a mature fashion what consequences may arise from this and to take pains that you will not be in a position of needing to suffer consequences. We wish from our hearts that God will grant you his protection and aid and that he will stand by you in all your good intentions.

We learned from Heinrich [Andermann?] that Müller has done everything possible to lighten your situation but that you did not accept it, which he considered very unwise on your part, and that it is your own fault if you persist in your opinion when Müller tried to do his best for you.[24]

No doubt some of Wright's letters outlining his total objection to involvement with the military have been lost. The only statement in the extant letters reflecting Wright's frustration during early 1863 is a brief passage in a letter from camp near Brooks Station, dated March 27, 1863. Wright tells David Silvan, "Up until now, there has been no change in my fate, for which I am really wishing, as I am fatigued by uncertainty. Still, the Almighty knows why it is going this way. Christ himself says that no hair may fall from our heads without it being his almighty will, and hence he will also receive us to himself, to his honor."[25]

David Silvan, Wright's most frequent partner in correspondence, wrote a touching letter whose tone appears to anticipate the forthcoming Day of National Humiliation, Fasting, and Prayer declared by President Lincoln for Thursday, April 30, 1863. Silvan's letter is identified as the "Duplicate of letter sent to E. B. W. Apr. 25th/63."

Esteemed Friend!

It is evening; a secret stillness surrounds the not-so-peaceful home front. In the garden, on the cedars and pines, the happy blackbirds are swaying, singing their evening song in shrieking stanzas. They are praising the Lord for being kept well during the day; they praise his goodness for feeding them without any worry on their part. Peace reigns in their circle.

Quiet twilight arrives and the weary workers hurry to the village. On the hill stands the chapel, whose little bell faithfully rings, sending afar its full, melodic tones to admonish the people to bring the almighty a loving song in his assembly hall.

But alas! It calls out almost in vain. The benches are so empty;

hardly any are there. The gray heads are only weakly, or not even at all, represented. Indeed, they have long since passed on to the eternal morning. How few of the aged are in the circle! The venerable, bald head of a loyal, courageous warrior for the kingdom of our God has only gathered a small group around itself. . . . [I]n the song, youthful voices are barely audible, and one asks: Where have they gone, who once filled and still should fill this room in the house of the Lord?

And so the hollow echo answers: Gone away! Away! Away! And if one asks about them, it sounds even more gruesomely through the night: Dead! Dead! Dead! They are to be sent into the ranks of those who, in their lives, may never have offended, yet in this tragedy we are all guilty, loaded with our sins, and hence we come to pray with the Psalmist and man after the heart of God: O Lord, rebuke me not in thy righteous anger, neither chastise me in thy displeasure, etc. [cf. Psalm 6:1, 38:1]. We nonetheless commend ourselves to the Lord and Savior, and give ourselves over to his discipline. Doubtless, he will make it right if we surrender our will. Yes, he wishes to be our leader in good days and bad, in joy and in sorrow.

The dear Creator has not ceased to give us joy again through his lovely springtime. Amidst the war, his springtime sun continues to rise over the just and the unjust. Ever and again, he shows his grace to those who live on earth; ever and again his father-voice calls: Come to me, all who are weary and heavy-laden. One does well to hear.

All nature rejoices in the pleasant warmth: even the gray-headed are leaving the long residence building in order to enjoy the pleasant warmth. Only one loyal head is missing [blank space, followed by a parenthetical statement in French wishing that the deceased may be allowed to rest in peace, and a statement in German that this is what any decent person would wish]. Still, the Lord granted him many a springtime, and if his spirit has passed through the clear blue ether toward eternal springtime, as the warm days come again and his grave-hillock is overgrown with green grass, if ever I might wish, I would wish to be with him.[26]

Eugene B. Wright may already have been on his way home from the military. It is not known precisely when he arrived back in Zoar, only that he did not accompany his unit when it left camp at Brooks Station, Virginia, in April 1863.

. . .

Only a few days later, Zoar commemorated the Day of National Humiliation, Fasting, and Prayer declared by President Lincoln for Thursday, April 30, 1863. It was most likely Wright who drafted the document, cited in the preceding chapter, explaining how the Zoar community used this occasion to justify its stance on patriotism. If that is so, then the fact that Wright and the Society of Separatists failed to achieve agreement on how to cope with the reality of military service did not keep Wright from defending the Society against allegations of disloyalty to its adopted American homeland.

It was around this time that the Society drafted an appeal on Wright's behalf to Secretary of War Edwin M. Stanton. Undated and marked *Concept* (draft version), the document does not show any indication as to whether it was ever sent, and if so, by which official(s) at Zoar, and what response—if any—it may have received. Following this appeal, though crossed out, is a statement concerning the history of Zoarite enlistment and doctrinal reasons for objection to war.

Edwin M. Stanton!
Sec. War, Washington, D.C.
    The subscriber (member of the Society of S. of Zoar, O[hio]) in the same of said Society, begs to represent to Your kind & friendly consideration, the following statement of facts, which most sincerely hope & trust will receive at your hands that attention which the nature of the subject in our opinion deserves.
    In August 1862, 10 young men (most of which were graduates of this establishment) volunteered their services to the U.S. (this rather a step in contra with our principles, which read thus: Thee [*sic*] shall not support the state by way of bearing arms against fellow-beings, for it being against the laws of our divine Saviour, however have allwaye [*sic*] been found willing to suffer such penalty as the State-Authority found proper to impose upon us; but in this case, it being the free will & voluntary act of those enlisted, it was admitted).
    After having been in the service for about 5 weeks, one of the above, with the name Eugene B. Wright member of Company I, 107 O.V.I. [Ohio Volunteer Infantry] became sick, and unable to perform the duty of a soldier; after 3 months sickness applied several times for a discharge, being convinced that he would never be in

that state of much usefulness to the Government—but in vain—was returned to duty by the Regimental Surgeon, but yet not compelled to perform duty, as being excused by his Capt. who himself considered him as unable to stand the hardships of a soldier's life. While in such a state, became convinced by reading the divine law in the N. Test. that he was entirely in the wrong way in comparison to our Saviour, and thus freely declared that he could not assist the business of War in no way [sic], and wished to be discharged on any terms whatever, but all in vain; he had to remain with said Rg. In such state without performing any kind of duty; although sick nearly all the time and seized with uninterrupted Rheumatism from Dec./62 to Apr./63, when the Reg. was ordered to leave their respective camp near Brooks Station, Va., being at that time not able to undertake a march, he was ordered by his Capt. to report at the Surgeon's Office, but was not accepted, & so was left in Camp subject to his own destiny, where he remained that day & night, & next day embarked on Steamer to Washington unmolested, from their [sic] took his way home per R.R. where he has since been treated as being afflicted with inflammation of the liver & Rheumatism, but yet convinced, not to use any kind of weapons (as being conscientiously opposed) towards human beings, according to the law of our Saviour—of the one—and entirely disabled by sickness to perform the duty of a soldier—as the other reason—to apply for a discharge.

As it is generally known, that the Secretary of War has authority to order or grant discharges, we took the liberty to address to You the above statement of facts, & trust & pray that through your kind influence & assistance, said E. B. Wright might get discharged from the service of the Army.[27]

On August 11, 1863, Dr. Carl Peter, of Winesberg (in Holmes County), Ohio, certified that "Eugene B. Wright a member of Comp. I 107 Regiment Ohio Volunt. [has been] since his return from his Regiment under my professional charge, he has been very severely afflicted with chronic Rheumatism and in consequences of it Hydrosis genu, he is not able to do any work nor to perform the duties of a soldier."[28] Perhaps anticipating that there might be some issues of credibility involving the certificate of Wright's medical status, N. F. Joss, who notarized this statement, added to it that Dr. Peter "is now & has been for a long number of years a regular

physician of this place, enjoys a large practice & the confidence of the
common city generally & as such his official acts in the profession are
entitled to full faith and Credit."

The next direct word from Eugene Wright comes from the Seminary
Hospital in Columbus, Ohio, in a letter to David Silvan dated September 1,
1863.

> On the 21st of August, I was brought, along with eight others, from
> New Philadelphia to Columbus, Ohio. We arrived here at 11:00 P.M.,
> and were taken to the guardhouse, where the others were locked
> up; praise God, I was not among them. The next day (Saturday) at
> 9:00 we were taken before the Provost Marshall who, as I believe,
> sent the others to their regiments. As for myself, he sent me to the
> superintendent of hospitals in Columbus, a Dr. Stanton, who treated
> me very amicably and asked me about my circumstances. I declared
> this openly to him, and he was kind enough to send me to this
> Seminary Hospital to be examined. This, however, did not take place
> until Thursday, as this is the only day on which examinations are
> conducted. The Board of Examination did not examine me much,
> as the Doctor of the Ward had earlier examined me; since he sits on
> the Board, he probably presented my situation to that group. The
> chief of the Board promised me with a smiling face that Papers of
> Inability to serve would be prepared, though I do not know when I
> shall receive them, hopefully soon.
>
> All in all, I could have wished for no better and friendlier treat-
> ment since being taken into custody, and here in the hospital I wish
> nothing more than to be declared free. If the doctor so chooses, it
> could take place soon.[29]

Finally, there are two undated items whose handwriting, style, and
specific content suggest authorship by Eugene B. Wright. The first appears to be a general letter that could be sent to various individuals, and
the content suggests that he wrote it to his former fellow soldiers following his return to Zoar.

> Friend N. N. [a convention indicating that one or more specific names
> may be added]
>   By the grace of our Savior Jesus Christ, I am in a position to

write to you from here. You may perhaps be more than a bit surprised; however, I believe that my condition is partially familiar to you, and how in fact I arrived here by God's fatherly protection. If I consider this, as I should, I can only wish that you yourself might experience such a great evidence of God's love, grace, and compassion, and that he might also lead you out of the slavery of the military as he has done for me, which no one thought possible.

How joyously, in my inner man, I set out on my way back, trusting in His protection, though not convinced whether I would be so lucky as to reach my goal. Still, I did not doubt, and could not, since our Savior himself does say: All things are possible to him who believes.

Supported by this and similar Biblical passages, I undertook this trip that was scarcely free of dangers. I arrived here happily under God's special protection, to the wonder of all who saw me.

All this redounded to the honor of God for those who rely on God and in this manner have already experienced his omnipotence for themselves—and perhaps to the annoyance of many who neither rely on Him nor wish to follow his commandments.

Still, I do not need to direct [or judge] myself according to this, but rather am bound ever to thank my Redeemer. I have now experienced for myself that He does not wish the death of the sinner, but rather that the sinner be converted and live. His grace is beyond measure. If he hears the meager prayers of a sinner, how much more will He hear those who have always taken pains to do His will.[30]

The remaining item may have been penned at many points in Wright's life. Because of the mention of a new year, it may have been a valedictory statement by Wright from early 1864, written a relatively short time prior to his death from tuberculosis on March 29, 1864.

My God, you have protected me in such a fatherly manner up to this point, kept me in the face of many a physical and spiritual danger, and since I can do nothing of myself, I ask you at the beginning of this year that you would further protect me from sin and other attacks; that you would bless my heart with wisdom, understanding, and the recognition of good and evil so that I may live my life to please you and benefit my fellow-man; and that you would not take me, in my sinful state, from this earth into speedy judgment. This I pray of you kind Father, for you alone are in a position to grant this to me. Amen.[31]

Eugene B. Wright died on March 29, 1864, but without the text of the funeral service, more information on his life and final days cannot be known.[32] In April, Wright's father remitted $10 in currency and $2.38 in "Change & Scripts & Stamps," presumably to settle any of his son's outstanding accounts.[33] Near the end of that month, on April 26, the Society paid Dr. Peter, who earlier certified the state of Wright's health, for "medical aid & medications furnished to E. B. Wright."[34]

Zoar's Other Volunteers and the Civil War

One of the most prolific correspondents during the early phase of Zoar's involvement in the Civil War was Christian Rieker.[1] His letters best reflect the experiences of a typical Civil War soldier trying to maintain ties with his home community. Their content, unpretentious and at times rather homespun, is totally genuine.

In a letter sent from Camp Cleveland on September 8, 1862, to his sister and brother-in-law, Rieker expressed the impatience of many soldiers eager to receive their first payments.

> We shall still be mustered today and receive our uniforms and money. If we do not receive what was promised us, we shall not go forward. All are unanimous and many have vowed not to go without their money.
>
> We'll not be in Cleveland much longer. I think we'll leave yet this week. If I can possibly do so, I shall come one more time before we leave, perhaps for the last time. Farewell.
>
> All the Zoar *volunteers* greet and thank all of you for the deeds of kindness that you have shown us.

A bit over a month and a half later, on October 19, 1862, Rieker wrote to his sister from Camp Delaware, Ohio. Some one dozen miles north of the state capital, Camp Delaware was located near a northbound route of the Underground Railroad. It was one of the few camps from which African Americans were deployed, and it is interesting to ponder whether Rieker may have met any African Americans while at this camp. While claiming that he had little news to report, he does document the active support and news network of those Zoarites who were traveling back and forth within the sites of the various camps.

Only a few days later, on October 22, 1862, Rieker wrote again from Camp Delaware, this time to his parents and siblings to tell them how he felt about having attained his age of legal majority while away from home and serving in the Union army.

> Since this is my birthday and indeed an important one, at least an important one for me—my 21st birthday—perhaps you are also thinking about it. To commemorate this 21st birthday of mine, I want to write you a few lines.
>
> I never would have thought I would spend a birthday—or this 21st one!—here and under these circumstances. For me it was a happy event simply to attain this age not attained by some of my siblings. I think they are better off than I [sie sind . . . besser ab als ich].
>
> But don't think that I am not happy, or that I cannot be happy, under the present circumstances. I simply mean that mine is a situation about which I have reservations [ein bedenklicher Stand]. How long I shall live or shall yet spend in this state is something I do not know. There is One who knows all that, as you yourselves realize, and we shall just allow Him to take care of the matter [und daher wollen wir nur ihn sorgen lassen].
>
> And now, we must once more move along. Yesterday we received marching orders, and we don't even know just when we need to get moving, or where we are headed. Some say we are going to Washington. . . . For my part, I believe we are going to join the troops commanded by Siegel. I don't think I can come home before I _._._._.: [punctuation sic].

Rieker then recounts an incident whose details agree strikingly with those reported by Jacob Smith in his memoir of service in the 107th Ohio, *Camps and Campaigns*.[2]

> Yesterday we buried a man. . . . He is from the 4th Ohio Regiment where Jähle also is. He died in the hospital and his father came and got him. He was already dead eight days when he was buried. His mother and the rest of his family were unable to view him. They couldn't open the casket because [of the state of his remains].

I think that tomorrow we are going to Mansfield [MS: Mains-field], Ohio, where we have to guard [prisoners?]. But it might also be that I could come home before then and visit you.

I am still healthy and well and wish the same for you.

With these few words I shall close my letter, hoping to find you well when we meet, sooner or later. Farewell, and do not forget me.

The letter concludes first in English, "Good By till I git to see you again / What I soon expect," and then in German he wishes his reader a good night.

Less than a month later, Rieker reports to his sister from Camp Ward, Virginia. The letter, on a leaf of the Charles Magnus stationery so popular at the time, is dated November 13, 1862.[3] The description of the nearby cemetery and references to the mortality rate for Rieker's fellow soldiers may have lent color to his letters, but it surely afforded little consolation to his readers back home.

We are now far separated from one another, about ten miles below Washington D.C., fairly close to the rebels.

They just rang the signal.

We had to dig entrenchments for four days, but you can imagine that we didn't strain ourselves.

We are close to Fairfax Seminary, a hospital with some two thousand ill patients inside. Every day, some four to six die. There is a nice soldiers' cemetery there where more than 200 lie, all having died in the last two months. All have a nice board on the grave on which is written the soldier's name, where he was from, and his regiment and company.

Last week I also sent a letter to you for all my siblings and our parents. I hope you received it. I cannot write as often now, though I never did write much, as I am so far away and do not always have the opportunity to send off the letters.

I recently received the letter that you included in Franz Strobel's letter.

There is much that I could write, but nothing is as good as recounting it in person, and there will be still more news to come.

When Eugene Wright returns [from medical furlough], send along a pair of gloves and a pair of underpants for me. And Thumm [MS: Thom] wants a shirt and also underpants, and John Kücherer would

In his letters, Christian Rieker mentions many family members whom he missed. One of these was his niece Salomena (Selma) Ruof, shown here as a young girl. Photo courtesy of Ohio Historical Society.

like a shirt, and John Geissler wants mittens and a shirt. Thumm and I would like mittens; Geissler would also like stockings. That is all that I know to ask you to send.

I hope you'll reply soon. I didn't receive any mail yesterday evening. All the others had a letter, and some two. When the mail arrives, everyone rushes together and listens attentively for the announcement of a letter, and makes all kinds of noise and shouts upon receiving a letter. It is a great joy whenever letters arrive. I would take one every evening if it just would come!

Now greet everyone for me, including niece Salomena and nephew Benjamen [elsewhere: Benjamin]. Write soon what Salomena is doing. I would like to see her again to find out whether she would still recognize me. I have to close my letter now. Greetings to Barbara Vetter and Barbara Bieler [Bühler, Beeler] and Barbara [Ruhle?]. Barbara Vetter sent me a few lines enclosed with my shirt. Tell her I've had no time to respond, but that I am grateful that she still thinks about me.

We do not hear again from Rieker until February 17, 1863, in a letter to his sister from Brooks Station, Virginia. Once again, he used stationery with a lithograph by Charles Magnus.[4] Although Rieker claims not to be much of a correspondent, a good number of his letters survive, and not uncommonly on rather nice stationery, considering the circumstances.

This letter is also important because of its news about the passing of Jakob Kümmerle (February 7, 1863, at Brooks Station, Virginia). Not for the first time, Rieker includes a reference to someone with a Zoar family who was no longer a direct affiliate of the Society. Both John Jähle (who had once lived at Zoar) and Huldreich Langlotz (whose association was through marriage) wrote letters to individuals at Zoar, indicating a tie to the community that extended beyond considerations of sectarian affiliation.[5] Facts such as these make a persuasive argument for including more names on the working list of "Zoar soldiers" than simply those of the 1861 and 1862 volunteers mentioned in the formal records of the Society.

Since I have time just now to answer your letter, I shall do so with joy. I suppose it is going for you as it is for me: almost daily I await letters with longing, but in vain I jump up whenever they say, "Letters, boys, letters." Everyone runs and converges. Still, I cannot expect that you should write to me every day, though the oftener the more pleasant it is for me, and the same is probably true for you as well.

Concerning the sick ones, we know nothing for certain, and I can write nothing about how they are doing. We are all still healthy and in good spirits, and I hope you are all still healthy, just as we are.

Jakob Kümmerle has died, as you may perhaps already know. It was very hard for us to see him die, so far removed from family and siblings, and in such a wild, rough, unfavorable area as it is here in Virginia. He is lying here alone, with just one comrade at his side in the wide, broad expanse that is perhaps an old cotton field. Though I do not think it will make much difference to a dead man, it looks quite uninhabited for those of us who must behold it. So now we just wish to grant him rest.

I also want to write you a bit about yesterday. Our new General Hooker[6] visited us yesterday, as he is now in [U.S. Major General Ambrose Everett] Burnside's place. So he held a review among all his troops and also came to our brigade to inspect us.

It was a source of great rejoicing among all the soldiers to receive General Hooker. Throughout the whole day yesterday, one didn't hear anything except music and cheers. As he approached, all his officers were accompanying him, such as Siegel, Stahl [MS: Stall], McLean, adjutants, and a host of others. There was a force of some fifty officers, and about 500 cavalrymen accompanying him.

When they came before us, the entire brigade gave *three cheers.* And when they were about in the middle of our brigade, General Siegel's horse fell from under him and was in such pain that it stumbled head-over next to Siegel, who could have died but was hurt only a bit on his arm. He mounted his horse as though it were nothing. His horse was also not injured. He took a hard fall, and it was miraculous that nothing serious occurred.

We had to bring our [battle] machines right past our commander to show him which was the best regiment. When it was all over, he praised ours and the 55th Ohio a great deal, but chiefly our regiment.

It was a beautiful day yesterday, as it is at home in May, nice and warm and pleasant. The birds were singing all around us. To look at it, it was just like a beautiful May day back home. But today it is winter again, snowing the whole day, and cold. . . .

Sunday, February 23, 1863. We really have to do a lot of *duty*. We need to make a road and two forts, all of which our division has to build. So farewell, write to me about [sister] Rika and how she is.[7] I don't know why she doesn't write to me.

The next (extant) letter from Rieker, written to his sister on April 12, 1863, from Brooks Station, Virginia, must have generated quite a bit of interest back home in Zoar because of its description of a review of the troops by President Lincoln himself.[8] It is unfortunate that the physical condition of the letter makes some parts virtually impossible to read.

Abraham Lincoln and his wife . . . visited the entire Potomac Army. . . . He visited each *corps* individually, and the generals were with him. The soldiers had to pass in review there in front of him, each corps in turn, especially the artillery and cavalry and infantry. It was quite something to see.

I believe that Franz [Strobel] is coming home; he can tell about it better than I.

I was also at Jähle's place last Monday. He is healthy and strong and sends his greetings to you, also to Benjamen and to you and Salome and Father. He is near Falmouth. They can see Fredericksburg from where he is, and the picket patrol of those tough-looking rebels.

I believe that if we go at it again, they will get *hell* from us; but will we get none?

Write me something about Rika if you know anything about her. Jahly [Jähle] told me that she had written him. . . . If you know anything about her, tell her to write to me if she can.

Also write me about Salomena and what she is doing. I believe she must already have grown just since I left. I don't think she would recognize me if I were to come home.

I'll see to it that I get there for a visit before we leave here, but only two per company may go at one time. When they return, then two more go. I do not know whether Franz is allowed to come home or not; it is still uncertain. Today we went down to Jahly and also to Leo [Kern].

Now I shall close with the wish that these few lines of mine may find you as healthy as I was when I sent them. Cordial greetings to

Benjamen and Father. I wrote him a letter last week; perhaps he has already received it. Greetings to John and Notter and Magdalena and Bielers and Dischinger and his wife and Gottfried, and Mary Müller's people, and Rauschenbergs, and [Lea?] and Groetzinger, and I don't know to whom all else.

If Franz comes home, I want to send along my letters. . . .

Georg Kümmerle is well again and also sends regards to Benjamen.

I also have not yet received the Box. I also want you to send a pillow back with Franz, but I would like you to keep that as much a secret as possible, as I already have too much to carry in my knapsack.

Some of Rieker's letters, while less notable in content, nevertheless reveal something about the day-to-day experiences of the Zoar volunteers. The following excerpts are from a letter sent by Rieker to one of his brothers on April 22, 1863, from Brooks Station, Virginia.

We are still here at the same old place and have not moved forward; as I had written, that was our intent. We would have done so if it had not rained so much. Now we need to be ready to march any day. We have here eight days' rations and need to conserve them. We shall have quite a lot to carry when we do finally get to move forward.

The drum has just sounded for picket, so I need to go, along with three days' rations, accompanied by Thom [Jacob Thumm] and A. Burkhart and Strobel and Leo, . . . I have not yet received the Box. Herewith I also want to send $10. Give them to Father, who will now have $100. For the time being, I want to keep the rest, as one never knows how things might go.

The next letter is far more sober in content. Rieker wrote to his sister on May 11, 1863, from his camp near Brooks Station, Virginia. He had been stationed there for some time, and no doubt his family members had their eyes fixed on the area. News of the Battle of Chancellorsville in the opening days of May 1863, Lee's astounding victory, the loss of Stonewall Jackson, and reports of some 30,000 soldiers dead, captured, or injured must have sparked nearly unimaginable anxiety in the hearts of Rieker's loved ones in Zoar. It is noteworthy that Rieker cites Psalm 91. Tradition maintained that each soldier who left Zoar as a volunteer in 1862 did so with a copy of that Psalm prepared by a loved one back home.

Dear Sister! With greatest joy I take up the pen in order to let you know again how I am doing and that I am still alive, and this is indeed a very great miracle. However, for God all things are possible. Just as is written in the Psalm [cf. Psalm 91:7–9], though a thousand fall on your left and a thousand on your right, it shall not strike you, for it is God who stands by your side to help you [dir beisteht], as I myself have now seen.

Many fell on my right and on my left, yet it did not harm me in the least. The bullets just whistled by [my] head like a true hailstorm; they simply whistled a little worse, as you can imagine for yourselves. Still, I sprang through it all like a rabbit, though I left my knapsack behind for the rebels.

Some even left behind their rifles and bread sacks. But you must not take this to mean that we were beaten. We simply got onto a good hill and then hung up the rebels with our twelve-pound cannons. That mowed them down like grass. The rebels fell like flies, often five or six deep, whole piles of them. Still, they did not give up until Monday, as they were all drunk as cows—which is what had given them their courage.

But they were beaten back. We took many rebels as captives, but they also took many of us as well. Even the rebels said that this was the hardest battle that they had ever had.

John Jahly was wounded, shot all the way through the mouth, in one side and out the other. He was taken to Washington. John Kümmerly [Kümmerle] is also missing. We don't know whether he is dead or taken prisoner by the rebels or perhaps just wounded. Nobody knows where he is. Fortunately, the rest of us came away unscathed.

In short, our Company I was about the most fortunate; only two companies remain larger than ours. There are some who have only 24 men; we still have 52 men.

And with this I wish to close. I think you can read all about it in the newspapers in greater detail: were I to write it all myself, I would need almost a week.

I wrote two letters, to Father and to John, in the form of a single letter. Since it is not possible to include everything in one letter, I told them that the letter was meant for all to share.

And, since I have time, I thought I would also write you a few additional lines. I hear that we shall soon be moving once more, so it could be a while until I can write again. If I am able to do so, I shall credit it to God and commit myself to Him.

If God wishes, I am ready to go, and as God wills, so it must be and remain. This I give as an observation, so that you do not think I have become despondent. As you might perhaps gather from my letter, it would be a mistake to think that I am.

Of course, I would rather see the war over, but not by our being beaten and the war thus ending. As is the desire of many: rather one more year as a soldier than to go the way of defeat.

Unfortunately, John Kümmerle had already died a few days earlier, on May 2, 1863, at the Battle of Chancellorsville. John Jähle fared much better, and a detailed account of his wounds appears in Jacob Smith's *Camps and Campaigns.*[9] Smith served in the ambulance corps that treated the wounded at Gettysburg. Though Smith does not give Jähle's name, the details coincide with those described by Rieker.

> Among the number brought back were some who were badly wounded. One in particular attracted my attention. He had been shot through the mouth, the ball entering one side of his cheek and out the other; in its passage through it had broken out four or five teeth and cut his tongue nearly off. He was shot through one of his arms and a musket ball had struck a small Bible which he carried in a pocket over his left breast, with sufficient force to go entirely through it, lodging and fastening in a bunch of eight or ten letters which were in the pocket between the Bible and his body; his escape was truly miraculous, as the ball came with sufficient force to have gone entirely through his body; the Bible in that case proved an effective shield.

Jähle is one of the less well-known individuals from Zoar. Beuter notes his departure from Zoar in 1861, and Rieker mentions him as a member of the 4th Ohio Volunteer Infantry. Nevertheless, Jähle's service record is elusive. Much of what is known about him comes from a sole extant letter sent from Camp Dennison, one of Ohio's largest training camps. The date is imperfectly given, either July 16 or—more probably for the 4th Ohio Volunteer Regiment—June 16; though no year is given, the service record of the regiment would indicate 1861. The stationery shows a picture of a locomotive, soldiers, and an encampment identified as "Camp Dennison near Cincinnati." The not-so-standard German shows consistent Swabian influences, as was true of the speech of most Zoarites but unusual for their written correspondence.

Dear Friend,

I've got to write you a few lines, but again, know nothing to write. I just wish I could have been with you for one more day, but had no time. Again, [the schedule was] too full. You know, man, I would gladly have been able to speak a few words with you damned guys, because it makes me mad every time I think about it, but it is my own fault.

You [plural] have said it to me often enough and I did not believe it, but [carrying?] the banner makes a fellow glad [macht Glück]. When I was still dying patterns [in the so-called Mustergewässer], I also had good times without animosity and contention, which I shall still have if I come away [from the war] with my life.

Unfortunately, I need to say that I could not be, nor would care to be, in Zoar any more; they got me to that point that I feel that way [sie haben es mir auch danach gemacht].

I would like to be with you young folks because I know that I still have good friends among you, but I have had a rich life since I left you the first time.

We got home almost the same day, in good shape. We left Wooster at 5:00 A.M. They were almost all folks from the city at the depot [Tibo]. We had quite a time as we got underway. There were plenty of tears and kisses.

We are still here in camp but do not know at what hour we shall need to go. Six thousand men from our camp are to go this week or next.

Now I wish to close my letter with the wish that it may find you healthy and doing well, as I am myself. Write as soon as you receive this letter. Greet your mother and siblings for me, and Jakob Rieker [MS: Rieger].
John Jähle

Tell Rose that the rose she sent me is very beautiful and was brought home healthy. If I come back to Zoar, I shall not forget it and shall repay [the favor].[10]

No doubt John Jähle returned from the Civil War with many reasons to consider himself a fortunate man whose friendship mattered to his fellow soldiers from Zoar and to the person(s) who wrote the "eight or ten letters" that backed up his Bible on a very fateful day in his life.

Returning to Christian Rieker, his last extant letter was written to his sister on May 30, 1863, from Brooks Station, Virginia. He was captured about one month later.

Dear Sister Märi Rouf, [11]

I received your last letter, dated the 17th of this month, in good order. I was so glad to read that you are all still healthy, as I myself still am, and as are the others, with the exception of Gottfried Kappel, who has been sick just about the whole time since we returned from our last battle. He has nervous fever [Nervenfieber: neurasthenia?] and is very sick. He is unaware of what is happening around him. Often he wants to leave, and when we ask him where, he says to Zoar. I don't have much confidence in his recovery, but we want to hope for the best. In general, quite a few are dying from the same illness in our regiment.

You wrote that I should report something about John Kümmerly, but I do not know where he is or whether he is still alive. It remains a question. If he were taken captive, at least we would know something about it. But there is no trace of him here. However, one shouldn't give up hope, as it could yet be that he was taken captive. Still, it also should not be a surprise if he were dead.

It is almost impossible to believe that as many as are still here came through the battle alive. Altogether we have lost only about 180 men. There are regiments that have lost 200 to 300 men. It especially cost us many officers: this time the rebels really filled their sacks.

Even our commander is in Richmond as a prisoner, as well as various others of our men.

You also wrote me that you had to laugh when you heard that we had to run so much [when under attack]. True, it is funny to hear about, but it wasn't funny any more for me when I had to run. I just had to pay attention to the bombs being shot at me. I pulled in my bulging [i.e., pack-laden] back whenever one came toward me.

I also let my backpack fly away, though I don't know how far it flew. Perhaps it is already in Tennessee with some rebel. I regret very much letting go of it, but at the same time, my life was dearer to me than my backpack.

And now I would like to know where our honest and loyal Eugene [B. Wright] is. He once said that it would not be right if he were a lieutenant and then went home. As we once said to him, he should become an officer and then he could resign and return home. But he did not think that it was right to do things that way, though it would have been better than breaking his oath and deserting, as he now has done. That shows his piety for what it really is. When he was here among us, he said it was a sin to kill, and so on and so forth. But he is not at all what I thought he was. He didn't even say goodbye to us. He just indicated that he didn't know if he would see us again.

In short: I must close now. I remain your Brother

Christian Rieker

[top margin, last page] I have lost my respect for Eugene. He is not a man.

As seen in the Society's letter to Secretary of War Edwin M. Stanton, Wright had already deserted and returned home to Zoar at the time this letter was written.

Christian Rieker was captured at the Battle of Gettysburg on July 1, 1863, and returned to his company on October 6, 1864. Rieker's sister, Mary, to whom he sent so many letters, wrote a letter to him dated December 5, 1864. Because Rieker was still in captivity and Eugene B. Wright (deceased March 29, 1864) was still alive when the letter was written, one must assume the correct date to be December 5, 1863. The original German is simple, highly colloquial, and tender.

Dear Brother,

I wish to take my pen with joy. For so long we thought you had been lost, fallen in battle. So far, we are all healthy. We were all so worried about you. On one occasion it was reported that you were severely wounded and still being held by the Rebels. This shocked me so badly that I could not close my eyes all night out of sheer worry, and just about everyone lamented. And just [as great] is the joy now [to have heard news of you].

Katharina Breimeier just brought me eggs as a greeting for you from her and her whole family. We added something to it in your

Many of Christian Rieker's letters were addressed to his sister Mary Ruof, shown here. Their sister Friederika was married to Huldreich Langlotz. Photo courtesy of Ohio Historical Society.

Box that you should boil until it is soft, not hard. You should only boil the "noodles" [Riwele] in the little sack a little bit in water or meat broth.[12] You don't need many to make a full kettle. We would not have sent so much cheese, but we thought that there would be others around you who were beset by hunger.

Annamaria Rauschenberger is sending you meat and the little [pieces of bacon?], Juliana Rauscheneberger is sending you gloves, and Rosina Rauschenberger helped me to bake crackers [MS: cracer]. All send you best regards.

Just now Franz Strobel is here on leave but must leave again by the 15th. He will also take along a Box, mostly with articles of clothing. If they send along something to eat, that is fine, but I am letting you know: I am so afraid that when you receive your Box you will eat too much [before your system adjusts to a normal diet], and everyone says that then there is nothing more that can be done to help you. I plead with you, dear brother, do not eat too much, and thank God from your heart that he has helped you thus far.

You are probably emaciated, but still you yourself will have to say that if he had not had his eye on you, you would have perished. If things are as reported in the newspapers, it is not any fun being a captured soldier.

And, if you are doing a little better, you can come here on leave for as long as is permitted. Both of our children have grown since you left and look forward to seeing you, and each says, "When my Christian comes, he has to sit down at the table with me." Salome says "Write a big greeting from me."

Friderika [the author and recipient's sister, Friederika Langlotz] also wrote. In Columbus they are in great fear because [General John] Morgan has escaped from prison there. He left a letter behind stating that he intended to return within four weeks to free his officers.

I know of no news to report other than that Magdalena had a daughter that died. Lea now has a son that is alive.

I think about how you are getting along as a prisoner, and no doubt you would have a lot to tell, so when you receive your Box, write to me immediately. I can hardly wait to receive a letter from you. . . .

Many greetings from me, Benjamin also sends greetings. Soon you will actually receive a letter from him.

If you find out anything about Leo or Lindeman, write right away.

Eugene Wright [MS: Eugien Reith] is now free from the military service. They took him to Columbus and he was exempted [MS: had become free] because of his illness. This summer he received all his property [MS: Gut; possibly an attempt by the author to express the concept of back pay?] since he enlisted.

He was doing rather well again, but now is doing so poorly that he cannot get out of his bed. They appointed him school teacher for

Friederika Rieker Langlotz and Mary Rieker Ruof, shown here in later years, were among the unsung heroines whose correspondence sustained their loved ones during the Civil War. Photo courtesy of Ohio Historical Society.

the small children, but he was not able to do even that because he was faring so poorly.

On January 31, 1864, Christian Rieker's brother-in-law, Huldreich Langlotz, described his own experience in the war and offered an assessment of Rieker's condition.

Chattanooga, January 31, 1864
Dear Father-in-law!

I just received a letter from my dear Friederika, in which she reported, to my joy, that she is healthy and doing well. She also sent me the letter that you wrote. That good soul! It appears that she wishes to make up for your not writing to me and says that I should not think ill of you for not being a great enthusiast about writing letters.

Now I won't deny that I was awaiting your reply to my previous letter, written to you last year in July—I still would like to know at least whether you received that letter. In your letter to my dear Friederike, I saw that, at any rate, you have not forgotten me altogether, and I thank you for your friendly inquiry concerning my welfare.

Thanks be to God, I am as healthy and strong as ever. Unfortunately, my appetite has been too good, relative to the small rations that we receive. Now, since the last battle in Lookout Valley, where our troops took possession of the railroad held by the rebels, we are once again receiving somewhat better rations. The train line is back in shape, and we now have rail connections open from Columbus, Ohio, to here.

Since my last letter to you, I have experienced so much more than I could possibly relate to you on paper. I shall just have to wait until I can tell it all to you in person.

Meanwhile, I have made it through three battles: at Hoover's Gap, at Chickamauga, and at Lookout Valley. Although the Battle of Chickamauga was the bloodiest and most tenaciously fought, I was fortunate enough to come through it, though a bomb did strike the ground about four feet to my right.

Toward evening, we were sitting around a fire, cooking a bit of coffee, when once more the rebels began to throw bombs into our lines. I barely had my little portion of coffee on the fire when this bomb came and struck the ground a short distance from us, though

without exploding. Within two minutes, we were all off to our se-
cure places of rest, where we laid ourselves down to sleep without
making any more fire, and without taking a bite of food.

This was on Saturday the 19th of September. On Sunday, the sun
rose as beautiful and warm, as though it wished to make amends
to those poor wounded soldiers who had to remain lying on the
battlefield and who had to spend the cold night there without any
kind of a blanket. Being Sunday, even the enemy appeared to want
to sanctify the day, and all hands were busy carrying the unfortunate
wounded soldiers from the battlefield into nearby houses where they
received medical assistance.

I don't wish to make it impossibly disgusting for you by describing the appearance of this battlefield. Here and there lay corpses
ripped apart by cannon fire, no longer similar in any way to a human body. We saw death in many different, grotesque forms that go
beyond all comprehension.

In the Battle of Lookout Valley, the bullets were whistling all
around me, yet none reached me, which sometimes still puzzles me.
God visibly held his fatherly hand of protection over me, for which
I daily thank him with all my heart. I also met Fidele [a.k.a. Leo]
Kern, who was still healthy and doing as well as when I last saw him.
I had not seen him, however, since our last battle here, and really did
not know where he was.

Because all our musical instruments were broken during the battle
at Chickamauga and we have not played since then, our command-
ing officer has decided to send us back to Camp Thomas, which he
will probably do in February.

At any rate, I shall then accompany my dear Friederike on the trip
to Zoar and shall be able to recount a great deal to you. Until then,
live truly well. Many, many greetings to you all, Father, Mother, and
siblings from your loving
Huldreich Langlotz
[immediately following on the same page] Dear John!

I shall also take advantage of this opportunity to write you a
couple of lines. First of all, I hope that these lines find you and your
family as well as I was when I wrote them, and if God wills, that our
poor Christian [Rieker] might be able to say the same for himself.

We do want to hope that he too can regain his health once more, and that we, after coming through these dangers and pressures, can see each other again.

I had this same sickness for almost two months and perhaps stood as close to the grave as he. Still, God heard my prayer and restored my health.

Also, the many beautiful letters from my dear Friederike kept my courage up and gave me strength. For a sickness such as this is not just physical, but rather for the most part one of weakened morale. After it has done what it can to weaken the body, it takes control of the mood to such an awful degree that one almost always has death in view. In this way, it turns into a disorder of the mood [Gemüths-krankheit] that soon wears down the physically weakened body.

For this reason, when you write encouraging and consoling letters to anyone who is so afflicted, you are providing an incredible source of help. So far, I have always maintained correspondence with my dear Friederike, and in eight months have received twenty-six letters. I have saved them all and they are all dear to me.

It would make me truly happy if you wrote an answer to this letter, and finally, I ask you to send me Christian's address. I really would like to write to him.

Cordial greetings to your dear wife and children from me. Farewell. Greetings from your brother-in-law,

Huldreich Langlotz

My address is:

H. Langlotz

Musician, 18th U. S. Infantry[13]

Chattanooga, Tennessee

Many greetings to Karl Cappel [Kappel] if you see him.[14]

Rieker came out of captivity and eventually returned to Zoar but evidently as a traumatized man. He married and became a father, worked as a blacksmith, and was an active member of the Society of Separatists. At age thirty-five he succumbed to Unterleibsentzündung (peritonitis?) and died Friday afternoon at 1:30 P.M., June 15, 1877, while in Canal Dover for his work. He was thirty-five years, seven months, and 23 days old, and according to the author of his funeral sermon, in "the best and strongest age" of life.[15]

Blacksmith John Beiter, shown here shoeing a horse while his daughter Helen watches, was still a youth when Christian Rieker returned from the Civil War. Perhaps he worked as a blacksmith alongside Rieker prior to Rieker's untimely death. Photo courtesy of Ohio Historical Society.

   The sermon text reports that the deceased, a Civil War veteran, returned from the military in a state of physical suffering. At first, things appeared to go better, but over time, and especially toward the end, things actually became worse. Rieker evidently sensed that his life's end was near and expressed that fact, though perhaps—according to the author of the sermon—he did not realize that the end was quite so near. The sermon's author recognizes this as a hard blow for the surviving family with its minor children but pledges the Society's aid and assistance to the widow and offspring. The choice of hymn and basis for meditation at the funeral service are appropriate for an occasion where faith is left wondering why things happen as they do.[16] It is difficult to read the text of this funeral sermon without concluding that its author somehow perceived that the deceased's difficult experience in the Civil War contributed—directly or indirectly—to Rieker's untimely death.

                                · · ·

Still another source of detailed serial narratives of the wartime experience comes from the letters of the Zoar volunteer John Geissler.[17] Injured in the service, Geissler eventually became a military nurse. In some ways, his experiences recall those of Jacob Smith, author of *Camps and Campaigns,* who was assigned to an ambulance unit. Geissler continued to correspond after being moved deep into enemy territory. He often named those whom he missed, such as Eugene B. Wright and Ludwig Heyd [Heid, Haid], and more than once asked David Silvan, a favorite correspondence partner, to share greetings via Silvan's extensive and active network of contacts. After the war, Geissler settled outside the Zoar community but even then managed to keep in touch with his old friends. Fortuitously, Geissler's extant letters begin just before Rieker's stop, and thus they form part of a continuum of correspondence from the field.

Geissler's earliest preserved letter, from "Aquia Creek Landing Eleventh Army Corps Hospital First Division," is dated "January the [blank] 1863." It appears to have been sent to a fellow soldier. The sale of a watch by Geissler is also mentioned by Eugene B. Wright in his correspondence, and Wright may have been the intended recipient of this letter.

Dear Friend,

I have already written one letter to you, but evidently you did not receive it. I really need some money. Send me a few dollars and some change as quickly as possible. If you get home before I return to the regiment, let Franz have your watch. Also, I would like to have ten dollars at home, in other words, if you get home, take that much of it home and give it to John Breimeier.

I do not know where John [Kücherer ?] is.

In a letter dated March 16, 1863, John Geissler wrote to Samuel Harr (Haar) from Mount Pleasant Hospital in Washington, D.C., to tell about his injury and pain.

My recuperation is progressing well, though my feet continue to hurt at night. Still, I can walk, and in other respects feel well. The care that we have here is good: we have good food and also good beds.

The items that you sent are doing me a lot of good, and I am thankful from the heart to you and to the entire Society.

I am still far from ready to serve and have no desire at all for the

Regiment, as [without rushing back to the military camp] I can still
lie on the ground a-plenty. I like it here, but if I could come home
for a while, it would do me good.

That same day, Geissler wrote to David Silvan, with much the same content and language of the letter just cited. A few additional passages from
this second letter, however, are worth citing.

It has been going a bit better all the time for me. Since I've been in
this hospital, I've improved significantly. When I came from Aquia
Creek, I could barely stand alone, and I couldn't walk alone at all. We
weren't well off there, but here we have good care, good food, and
good beds. Everything has to be completely clean, and every Sunday
there is an inspection.

My feet still don't want to walk, and at night they still hurt me a
lot; I'm still a long way from being ready for service.

By autumn of 1863, John Geissler reported that he had stayed on at the
same hospital, though now as a nurse at Mount Pleasant General Hospital.
With some fifteen hundred beds at various periods, Mount Pleasant General
Hospital in Washington, D.C., was one of the largest Civil War hospitals.
Geissler also makes one of several references by Zoar's soldiers to their involvement in musical activities. Considering the community's rich heritage
of musical performance, this is scarcely surprising.

Mount Pleasant General Hospital Washington D.C. Ward No. 6
October 6, 1863
Esteemed Friend!

On this occasion I want to report to you again how it is going for
me. I was transferred last week to Ward 6 as a nurse. I am no longer
in the tents; we have it harder here, and we have a lot of work. There
are thirty-two beds in each ward, with five nurses [per ward?]. I need
to stay up all night long, but still, it is better than in the field.

There are ten wards in the building, and each ward is 100 feet
long, and in the front of the building are medical stores and the doctors, and the office. Water is driven by an engine into all the wards
and piped around. It is installed very well.

I thought I could pay you a visit when I wanted, but I heard that we have to be here during the night. You can count on the fact that [the anti-Lincoln political candidate Clement Laird] Vallandigham isn't getting my vote. To get a furlough here is a complete impossibility if one isn't wounded; there are people here who try everything possible, who are lying here ill and of no further use to Uncle Sam. . . . No furlough is given here except for the wounded or to save a life; when one is not ill, there is no possibility of receiving one, unless one has a good friend who helps him out. In actuality, the reason is perhaps because almost half would not return.

Last week we had a major inspection here. They took all the men who are fit for the Regiment, and took mine as well. A great number were sent out. They are still keeping us nurses here. It appears that that is how it is supposed to be, and that I am not supposed to get out of here. I know that the doctor who has charge over our ward will not send us out, unless it has to be, and then only by force.

I could have been transferred to a Band if I were in an invalid choir, but that is not possible. The doctors here also wanted to organize one and get a teacher from up north, but whether it will go that far, I am not certain. I don't think the money will be forthcoming: that's what the matter is!

As far as I am concerned, I am healthy and well; things continue to be fairly lively here, [and] Old Ab[raham Lincoln] looks pretty cheerful again since things have taken a better turn.

In a letter Geissler wrote after his deployment deep in the South, in South Carolina and Florida, he describes the Battle of Legareville, a battle often cited because of the decisive role played by the steam gunboat USS *Marblehead*. It was also one of the battles in which a large number of African American soldiers distinguished themselves in the Union military forces.

Coles Island, South Carolina[18]
1st Brigade. Gorden's [*sic*] Division.
January 8, 1864
Worthy Friend!

I received your esteemed [correspondence] in good order via Franz Strobel, and hence want to report right away how it is going for us.

As far as health is concerned, we are—thank God—all healthy and doing well. We hope and wish the same for all of you.

Early last Christmas morning, the rebels made an attack on our gunboats but were driven back and in part had to leave behind their artillery. They wanted to come over to our island since only the Stone River separates us. On the U. S. gunboat *Marblehead*, two men were killed and five wounded. Still, we don't need to march so much, and we like it rather well here.

We have fairly cold weather and a lot of rain, after which it always turns cold.

Now and again we also get deserters from the rebels. They say that many would come over to us if they did not have families in Charleston. Even they believe that they will need to give up soon. When they have opportunity, they also exchange newspapers with our people. Still, we believe the war will come to an end this year, if that is God's will.

The following correspondence to John Sturm, dated January 18, 1864, originated at Coles Island, in the same general offshore area of Geissler's other correspondence from South Carolina. The letter is noteworthy not only for its news from the front but also for its mention of the active and ongoing communication between Zoarite soldiers, evidence of which appears in the letters of virtually all members of the Zoar cohort.

Your letter made its intended way to my hand via Franz Strobel, and it made me very happy to hear something from you again. I am glad that all of you are healthy and well. Thanks be to God, I can enjoy my good health, and all the others are also healthy.

We received your Box in good shape and really thank you for everything, which was all in good condition.

Concerning the news of the war, you've surely learned from the newspapers that things are taking a slow course. I don't believe that they can get Charleston from this side since they don't even have Sumter yet.

We have to do a lot of picket duty here, each time staying out two days and two nights.

A lot of Ohio regiments have reenlisted again as veteran soldiers for three years, since their time was up.

Still, we are hoping that in this year just begun, we'll have better successes for the North and won't need soldiers for another three years, though it appears that the South is not of a mind to give up until they have been completely beaten. They still believe that they can become independent from the North.

Indeed, by the time another year had passed, William Tecumseh "War Is Hell" Sherman had completed his famous march to the sea and in early 1865 turned his attention to South Carolina, specifically Charleston Harbor and Fort Sumter. Long before then, however, Geissler had been deployed elsewhere.

As a rule, Geissler's letters are dated fairly soon after a change of location. If for no other reason, such promptness by Geissler enhanced the likelihood of a timely response from Zoar in the form of further correspondence and packages. The following letter is dated March 5, 1864, soon after the arrival of Geissler's unit in Jacksonville, Florida. As in most of his letters, Geissler shares detailed observations on the course of the war.

We left [offshore South Carolina] Folly Island February 28 and sailed to Florida on the steamer *Delaware*. Tuesday we left, and arrived Wednesday noon in Jacksonville, Florida. We have really fortified ourselves here. We are building a large fort, and the Rebels cannot repel us from here. We also have a lot of gunboats here and continue to fear an attack, but the rebels don't have the confidence. They'll be smart to stay away, if they don't want to get their fingers burned.

However, we cannot move ahead either. It would be just as hard on us, as we are insufficient in numbers. Deserters come over to us almost daily; even women have come to us.

The little city is rather pretty, but a great deal has been destroyed. All in all, we rather enjoy it here. No doubt it will get terribly hot here this summer. All the fruit trees are already blooming here . . .

We've received flour a couple of times because they didn't have anything else. At the beginning, our ration was rather meager. I just wish you could have seen how we baked cake for ourselves. One fellow had an old shovel and another a rusted can and some put the dough on pieces of bread and held it to the fire. In the beginning, we didn't even have salt. That was quite a story. If one is hungry, one can make do with anything; this is especially so for the soldier. When I come home, I'll be able to eat everything. . . .

We all wish that this Humbug War would come to an end. We

heard yesterday evening that [Gen. Nathaniel P.] Banks is supposed to
have taken Mobile, but whether this is so I do not know. I do think
it likely, however, that the Rebellion will come to its conclusion this
summer. I believe that perhaps we could be here a while, as we are
supposed to be here only to maintain the location. We are too weak
to move forward. This week, Gilmore also held review with us.

Geissler then shares a long list of friends in Zoar, and even of former Zoarites, to whom he extends his greetings.

The last letter from John Geissler was sent to David Silvan from Marysville, Ohio, after the conclusion of the war, on January 29, 1869. In this
letter, Geissler expresses condolences for the untimely passing of Silvan's
wife. It is three years since Geissler has seen Silvan, and he would dearly
love to see him and speak with him again. Things are going well for
Geissler, though he does report that his business partner has left and that
they sold the shop. Geissler also wonders how the cobbler shop in Zoar is
doing since he left. Money is scarce in the Marysville area. Although he
has had some good times with the local girls, as "an elegant man among
the ladys [sic]," Geissler concludes that he will be better off if he remains
single. He also tells of a jolly time at an oyster supper following an initia-
tion of the Odd Fellows some thirty miles away in Columbus. He concludes the letter with many greetings.

The smaller corpus of letters from John Brunny [Brünne, Brunne] Jr. and
Franz [Frank] Strobel fill in many of the details not included in the letters
of Rieker and Geissler. The first of Brunny's letters was sent from Camp
Wallace, Kentucky, and is dated September 25, 1862.

Esteemed Friend, [because I have always valued you as a good friend,
I also consider it my duty to portray to you a day in our adventurous
life as soldiers, namely, the first significant march that we took. This
occurred on September 23. At 9:00 A.M., we received the order to
march, whereupon we immediately packed everything and marched
off right away. We headed from our previous encampment at Covington, Kentucky, toward the southwest, as we were supposed to
move into the camp recently vacated by the 104th Ohio Regiment.
At first, things moved forward, accompanied by song [unter Sang
und Klang] until the dust prevented our singing. For there arose

such massive dust clouds that we could not see three steps in front of ourselves.

Finally thirst also set in, as we had no water with us, and the great heat caused by our heavy packs increased the weakness of our human powers to such an extent that after only three miles, dozens were looking to the fence corners [Fenzecken], from which they were immediately driven off by the officers.

During the march, I often saw soldiers bend down to the dirty puddles [Drecklachen] to scoop up water, but instead of getting water, they just got a muddy mass that could scarcely be designated as water. After four miles of marching, we arrived at the camp of the 102nd Regiment, where we rested a bit. Then we moved ahead.

All around here, protective entrenchments [Schanzen] have been thrown up and trenches opened. Also, many 12-, 24-, 32- and 36-pound cannons have been positioned that will be sent against the rebels' pretty blue beans if they sense any desire to show themselves at close range.

From here [the intended destination] was said to be only one quarter of a mile. Upon this assurance, we set out courageously again, but when we put one quarter of a mile after another behind us and still had not arrived, most lost courage and again broke ranks, despite the captain's cursing.

The longer the lack of order lasted, the greater it became. One could see whole rows lying exhausted along the road. Several fell down unconscious on the slope of the hill, overcome by sunstroke, from which one of them soon died.

Finally, at two o'clock, after having covered eight miles, we reached our camp. But scarcely half of us arrived then, and hundreds more only after another two or three hours. And many are still ill now.

To our greatest dismay, we only then realized that the entire march was an exemplary masterpiece of stupidity and inability on the part of our leaders, for the place where we now are located is barely two miles away from our previous camp and could have been reached in one hour.

Our camp is on a hill crowned by cannons. . . . From here one might clearly see Cincinnati. Now because of the space [on the page], I must break off [this letter]. Also greet M. Miller and R. Arnold. I am looking forward to an answer soon.[19]

It is a little surprising that other Zoarite soldiers did not mention the march that is the main topic of this letter, though other letters describing it may simply no longer be extant. Smith, in *Camps and Campaigns,* describes this march less circumstantially, albeit with equal disdain for the useless expenditure of energy. Smith does, however, add the intriguing detail that the German Americans of Company F restored morale by leading a song whose chorus included the lines (as they sounded to his Anglophone ears), "Und de bix a mis a knolla / Und de rebels mis a folla / In de Sout, in de Sout, in de Sout" (And the rifles have to crack / And the rebels have to fall / In the South, in the South, in the South).[20]

Brunny's next letter comes from Stafford Courthouse, Virginia, located in the same county as George Washington's boyhood home. Dated December 28, 1862, it gives a succinct yet vivid picture of reduced troop strength, and of camp food.

> Our Regiment is divided into Gen. MacLean's Brigade, which is in Gen. Stahl's Division. The regiments near us are all reduced, most of them consisting of only 200 to 300 men. The 9th Ohio, a la Mill Spring, has only 140 men capable of bearing arms; our regiment as well has been reduced, from 935 to 650; most of the rest lie in the hospitals in Washington and Baltimore.
>
> As for food, we really have enough. I'll remain quiet about the quality, since the very word "Crackers" sickens me.[21] Yesterday again we received two potatoes per man, something we'd not had in some time.[22]

The next letter from Brunny affords a complement to the descriptions of the battle offered by John Geissler. It is sent from Camp on Folly Island, South Carolina, and is dated December 25–29, 1863. Union troops began occupying Folly Island in 1863; eventually, some 13,000 troops were stationed there. Its location is proximate to South Carolina sites mentioned in correspondence by other Zoar soldiers, such as John Geissler.

> In my tent, as I lay in the morning in Morpheus's sweet arms, F[ranz] Strobel surprised me, shaking me out of my sleep to give me a deluge [Sündflut] of letters, among which was also your highly esteemed letter.
>
> I sat up at once—I didn't need to get dressed—and read through them all with the customary haste with which the soldier reads about

The cider wagon was a welcome sight for thirsty workers awaiting their mid-afternoon refreshment. Photo courtesy of Ohio Historical Society.

the news from home. I had been waiting for a long time for a letter from you but thought you'd have little time for writing letters this summer. A job, such as Frank described the cider press as being, must certainly have demanded a lot of hard work and time.[23]

I often wish I could just have been there when you were at work last autumn, but that couldn't be, and so now with that I shall give you the short description of this area that you wanted.

The port of Charleston is surrounded by many small islands: Morris Island, Sullivan's Island, Folly Island, James Island, Cole, Kiawah, Seabrook, and still many other small islands.

Morris Island is nothing but a big sandbank. There isn't a single tree on it. That is also how one half of Folly Island is, whereas the other half is grown over with pines, laurels, palms, and a strange sort of oak tree, as well as a lot of underbrush [Unterholz] and climbing plants [Schlingpflanzen].

This island is approximately six miles long, but only one-half mile across, and is loaded with sand hills and swamps. The camp of the troops here lies on the sand hills along the seacoast. Still, the troops need to switch every month because every day the ocean washes away some three feet of the island so that one is in danger of being inundated by the sea.

On the north end of the island lies General [Quincy Adams] Gillmore's headquarters, surrounded by defensive entrenchments whose defenders frequently engage the rebels. On the northern tip is a landing and harbor for large steamers and vessels, a number of which always lie here at anchor. This landing is surrounded by five forts armed with 32- and 64-pounders.

From the sand hills, one has beautiful vistas of the city of Charleston and all the fortifications, and we can clearly see the bombardment. [Fort] Sumter, to me, resembles a pile of stone and dirt because when one of Gillmore's 300-pound [sic] defensive artillery pieces hits it, a cloud of sand, rocks, and mortar will sometimes fly 40 feet in the air, and then wagonloads of the stuff slides into the water.

The city is mostly bombarded at night, something that is dreadful to watch, yet at the same time, uncommonly beautiful. One can follow the bombardment shells with the eye, from the firing to their descent and explosion.

For the rest, we don't have a pleasant stay here: the water is bad and briny; the food is bad.

The 107th OVI lies on Cole Island, about a mile away from Folly Island. They are about a mile from the town of Legareville, the site of a sharp encounter a few days ago [December 25, 1863].

During the night, the rebels planted six 64-pounders right near our pickets and gunboats, upon which they fired violently at daybreak. The warships *Pawnee*, *Marblehead*, and a mortar boat shot away at them in such a manner that they immediately got out of there, leaving two of their 64-pounders, as well as all their munitions, bread bags, and other items. A lot of these lay scattered about, for the bomb splinters [sic] had come too close. Our total loss consisted of two dead and five wounded.

Our brigade [illegible] consists of six regiments divided across three islands: Folly, Cole, and Kiawah (two miles from Folly). We have to play every day for a regiment, also for General Gorden [sic] and Schimmelpfennig [MS: Schimmelpfoenig], a night owl. And so we are always on the go, via steamboat, often reaching home at 12:00 P.M.

Photograph from Zoar of an unidentified bugler who may be John Brunny or Huldreich Langlotz. Photo courtesy of Ohio Historical Society.

Our band consists of twenty men. Since only two of us blow the lead part [da wir aber nur zum zweit Lead blasen], you can understand that it is not so very easy, with uniform on, parading around [herumstolzieren] until the lips are sore. That, at least, is past, because the skin becomes thick as leather if one does nothing for a year and a half but blow. Earlier, however, it was terribly bothersome [plagend übel].

Right after the Battle of Chancellorsville [May 1863], I wrote to D. C. Hall in Boston and had a very beautiful and good silver horn sent. Though it cost me $45, it has the newest *movements* , rotary valves, but with some improvements.

Something else: we who are members of the band of the 107th have several times asked the general, for certain reasons, [that we be allowed] to return to the regiment, but so far the general has not consented. We are hoping, nonetheless, to be back with the regiment in a few weeks. Our colonel promised [to intervene] for us. In the regiment we need to play only half as much and also do not need to play at the whim of every monkey in shoulder straps.[24]

In his last extant correspondence, Brunny, signing the letter "Your former brother-wind-instrumentalist," wrote on July 28, 1864, from Fort Clinch, Florida, to David Silvan. A masonry structure on Amelia Island, Fort Clinch was occupied at various times by both Union and Confederate forces.

I've been playing in the minor key of my life for two years now, and it will take another year until it is all over. Still, I must admit that, alongside many discords, it also has many a charming tone. . . .

But enough of this. There is not much new, except that we continually have a true African heat down here in swampy Florida, and that the mosquitoes are so thick that one can scarcely walk.

Music is made all day and often at night so that we are not very bored. It is just that we lack pieces of music, and the Plague Spirits, our officers, want to hear new pieces each day. [25]

Finally, there are three extant notes from Franz Strobel.[26] Strobel was born in 1840, came to the United States in 1854, and entered the military service in 1862, when already married but not quite twenty-two years of age.[27] He was promoted to corporal on December 1, 1862, and to sergeant July 1, 1863.

Frequent references in the letters of Rieker, Geissler, and Brunny suggest that Franz Strobel played an active role in the communication network of the Zoar soldiers. Though brief, Strobel's correspondence shows a concern for keeping accounts in order and for giving proper recognition to those who have earned it. No doubt such attention to detail helped Strobel in his capacity as a sergeant of Company I, where he had special opportunities to facilitate communication among the men under his charge, especially among his fellow Zoarites.

Along with the first of his extant letters, written at Brooks Station, Virginia, on June 6, 1863, Strobel sent $50 to David Silvan and asked him to "divide the enclosed as follows," indicating that $30 was from Gottfried Kappel (who died in the war on June 12, 1863) for Kappel's father, $15 from Leo Kern to Levi Bimeler, and $5 from John Kücherer to John Breimeyer.[28]

On March 3, 1864, Strobel wrote to Silvan from Jacksonville, Florida, with the request, "Please let my wife have as much Cash as she may need. Charge to my acc[ount]. With respect yours, Francis Strobel in haste."[29] As a matter of fact, Strobel—and from time to time his wife—were among the most active users of the Society's general account that handled the finances of soldiers away from the home community.[30]

Strobel wrote another letter to Silvan from Fort Clinch in Jacksonville, Florida, dated June 2, 1864:

Herewith I send on to you five Memoirs, each with its respective name on it. Be so good and give them to the closest kin of each. Since each costs only $1.50, I have decided to take one as well for [the late] G[ottfried] Kappel
[then, in English] P.S. Please tell my Wife to get mine fraimed & a glass over it in order to ceep it clean & charge me with all the extra Postage it may cost.[31]

A final mention of Franz Strobel in the extant correspondence comes from the physician Ben Feucht, writing to David L. Silvan from Beaver, Pennsylvania, on November 15, 1866.[32] Feucht asks if Strobel is still in Zoar and requests eight measures of the best cashmere for a Sunday suit, as well as a selection of styles. If Strobel is no longer in Zoar, Feucht prefers to let the matter go rather than incur special charges.

Though Franz Strobel did return to Zoar, tragedy stalked his family. He lost both a young son and a foster child at Zoar during his postwar years. Strobel eventually moved to Stark County, where he died in 1914.

The Aftermath

Neither Eugene B. Wright's outspoken rejection of war nor the sentiments of those young men who objected in writing to the war and subsequently paid fines for nonattendance at militia muster were able to stem the tide of an irreversible change in Separatist thinking. Though Zoar's volunteers may have constituted less than a majority of the community's young men, the fact remains that more men enlisted than were "bought free" from the military through the payment of bounty money.

As the war took its course, the Americanization of Zoar continued apace. Not so very long after the Civil War, *Harper's New Monthly Magazine* published in its July 1870 issue a fanciful piece about Zoar by Constance Fenimore Woolson.[1] Titled "The Happy Valley," Woolson's piece presents Zoar as a quaint and rather anachronistic enclave of simple yet goodhearted folks. What is interesting in the present context is not the content of "The Happy Valley" itself but rather the author's response to criticism that she portrayed the residents of Zoar in an unfavorable light. In a letter dated July 20, 1870, she apologized to David Silvan, stating that the *Cleveland Herald* had republished her story without her knowledge or consent. Had that not taken place, the people of Zoar might never have known what she wrote. Nevertheless, she did make it clear that Zoar was no longer the little German town of romantic imagination. "The readers of 'Harper' [sic] would not care for an account of Zoar as it is now, almost entirely Americanized; but they would all be much interested in a description of the place as it was twenty-five years ago when all the differences of dress, language, manners &c &c were so much more marked than they are now, and the place seemed like a foreign town."[2] No doubt Zoar's participation in the

A Zoar villager, identified in another photo as Civil War veteran Anton Burkhart, poses in front of a United States flag on which one can read names of Zoar men who served in the Civil War. Photo courtesy of Ohio Historical Society.

Civil War was but one element in the mix that produced this irreversible change in the practices and perspectives of Zoar's residents.

On October 7, 1877, David L. Silvan passed away. He had suffered from a wasting disease for twelve years, during which time he had experienced the death of his own beloved wife, Paulina. William Bimeler noted in his compendium on October 8, 1877, that Silvan had for a year endured the most difficult bedfast battle for his health that anyone in Zoar ever recalled having witnessed. The text of the funeral service names Silvan (deceased at age thirty-eight) as then being one of the youngest members of the Society and declares that his presence would be sorely missed.[3] By that point, any relatively young departing member of the Society would be sorely missed.

Silvan's death represented both the passing of a truly loyal Separatist opposed to bearing arms in the Civil War and, at the same time, of an important human link between the soldiers and the community back home in Zoar. It was he who corresponded most with Zoar's soldiers and who (for example, in the case of John Geissler) enjoyed contact even after a

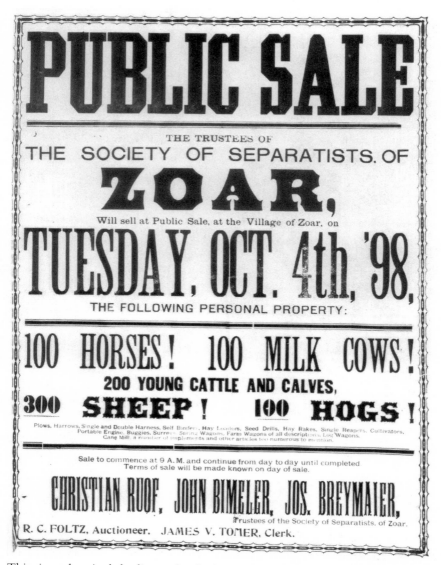

PUBLIC SALE

THE TRUSTEES OF

THE SOCIETY OF SEPARATISTS. OF

ZOAR,

Will sell at Public Sale, at the Village of Zoar, on

TUESDAY, OCT. 4th, '98,

THE FOLLOWING PERSONAL PROPERTY:

100 HORSES! 100 MILK COWS!

200 YOUNG CATTLE AND CALVES,

300 SHEEP! 100 HOGS!

Plows, Harrows, Single and Double Harness, Self Binders, Hay Loaders, Seed Drills, Hay Rakes, Single Reapers, Cultivators, Portable Engine, Buggies, Surreys, Spring Wagons, Farm Wagons of all descriptions, Log Wagons, Cane Mill, a number of implements and other articles too numerous to mention.

Sale to commence at 9 A. M. and continue from day to day until completed
Terms of sale will be made known on day of sale.

CHRISTIAN RUOF, JOHN BIMELER, JOS. BREYMAIER,

Trustees of the Society of Separatists, of Zoar.

R. C. FOLTZ, Auctioneer. JAMES V. TOMER, Clerk.

This sign advertised the livestock sale that was part of the formal dissolution of the Society of Separatists in 1898. Photo courtesy of Ohio Historical Society.

former soldier left Zoar to live elsewhere.

In later years, Zoar veterans reconvened (as seen in a photo near the beginning of this study) wearing the medals of the Grand Army of the Republic. Perhaps the occasion for the reunion was the Ohio Centennial

Elizabeth Beiter is shown here beside the water pump on September 21, 1930, at age 79. Her life (1851–1944) spanned more than nine decades, and she was able to offer interview data for Edgar B. Nixon's 1933 dissertation on Zoar. Photo courtesy of Ohio Historical Society.

Exposition in 1888, when a parade by this group of veterans marked the opening of festivities celebrating the 100th anniversary of the first settlers arriving in Ohio.[4] About the same time, a picture was taken of the man identified in the photo of Zoar's veterans as Anton Burkhart, who stands beside a small child and a young adult helping to display a U.S. flag emblazoned with the names of Zoar soldiers who served in the Civil War. Perhaps on this occasion Burkhart or other veterans recounted their adventures to an excited young audience.

Zoar—already in a challenged state as a religiously based experiment in communal living at the time of the Civil War—had shed its historically pacifist stance and had thereby taken still another decisive step toward inevitable integration into mainstream American society. In 1898, approximately one generation after the conclusion of the Civil War and perhaps

Joseph Breymaier, along with John Bimeler and Christian Ruof, presided over the dissolution of the Society of Separatists in 1898. Like that of Elizabeth Beiter, this photograph of Joseph Breymaier dates from 1930. Photo courtesy of Ohio Historical Society.

one decade after the photograph was taken of Zoar's veterans wearing their medals of the Grand Army of the Republic, the Society of Separatists was formally dissolved.

A system was implemented for distribution of property among remaining members and those deemed eligible, by birth and residence, for a share in the settlement. Since the Society had long ceased to function with its original idealistic fervor, many residents no doubt continued to live more or less as they did prior to dissolution. For at least a period of time, the distribution of shares of property assured awareness of who—or at least of

whose family—had once been active in the Society. Even today one sometimes hears the term "descendent" in reference to a person whose ances-
tors were members of the Society, and specifically, to those whose families
shared in the settlement of 1898.

By the time the Society of Separatists disbanded, the authors of the letters cited in this study had died, moved away, or were no longer fully active
affiliates of the Society. The three Zoar veterans photographed with their
medals of the Grand Army of the Republic, however, provided a continuing link to the Civil War experience. Anton Burkhart, who died in 1922,
enjoyed many years in which to impress young and old with his recollec-
tion of having seen President Lincoln in person; John Kücherer, who died
in 1926, could tell about his dramatic rescue by an African American; Leo
Kern, who died in 1921, was a survivor of the horrors of the prison at Andersonville.[5] As fate would have it, these three former soldiers from Zoar
whose letters have not survived—if indeed there ever were any—remained
after the dissolution of the Society to share their memories and to commemorate Zoar's involvement in the Civil War.

Notes

An Overview of Zoar in the Civil War

1. For the background in the European homeland of the movement that led to the formation of the Society of Separatists of Zoar, see the two-part article by Eberhard Fritz, "Roots of Zoar, Ohio." A Zoarite's overview of these events appears in Philip E. Webber, "Jakob Sylvan's Preface."

2. Still indispensable because of the many primary documents it includes is E[milius] O. Randall, "The Separatist Society of Zoar." Also foundational in its use of archival sources, especially those written in German, is Edgar Burkhard Nixon, "The Society of Separatists of Zoar." Two popular accounts worth consulting are Hilda Dischinger Morhart, *The Zoar Story;* and the Ohio State Archaeological and Historical Society (now the Ohio Historical Society), *Zoar: An Ohio Experiment in Communalism.*

3. For the destruction of Sodom and Gomorrah, see Genesis ch. 19. Biblical Zoar is described as being unusually lovely, known for its palm trees (Gen. 13:10, Deut. 34:3), and the place to which the besieged Moabites were told to flee (Isa. 15:5, Jer. 48:34). The Amana Inspirationists, with whom the Zoarites maintained contact and often are compared, practiced communitarianism for ninety years (1842–1932), though in two widely separated locations: initially near Buffalo, New York, and in nearby Canada, and later in Iowa. Ephrata Cloister in Pennsylvania is one historical communal society that claims a longer history than Zoar, albeit under remarkably different circumstances. By any standard, however, Zoar's historical longevity is indeed noteworthy.

4. A leader in the Communal Studies Association, Fernandez is currently engaged in active research on Zoar that holds great promise for further understanding of the community and its practices.

5. Kathleen M. Fernandez, *A Singular People,* 167–71, gives a comprehensive list of individuals who provided first-person accounts of life at Zoar. Among the more widely circulated accounts were those of William Alfred Hinds, *American Communities,* 91–123; and of Charles Nordhoff, *Communistic Societies of the United States,*

99–113. Not a first-person account, but based heavily on such material, is Mark Holloway, *Heavens on Earth*, 88–100.

6. Webber, "Jakob Sylvan's Preface," esp. 122.

7. Ibid., and Fritz, "Roots of Zoar."

8. At the risk of bypassing some of the rich literature on German Americans and their opposition to slavery, I would like to point to one recent and perhaps underutilized resource dealing with one segment of Ohio's German Americans: Alexander Richter, "Slavery, Abolitionism, and Race."

9. One useful preliminary bibliography on the individual units from Ohio is www.ohiocivilwar.com. For Cincinnati's Neuner, see also Constantine Grebner, "*Die Neuner.*"

10. To cite but one example, chosen because it is affiliated with a publisher (Verlag für Amerikanistik) and hence less potentially ephemeral: www.bigcountry.de.

11. Janet Hickman, *Zoar Blue,* 139

12. See, for example, the roster of Zoarite soldiers in Hickman, *Zoar Blue,* 42.

13. Ohio Historical Society, MSS 110 AV. See pp. 5 and 6 of the typescript Inventory of that manuscript collection for a list and brief description of other Zoar-related resources held by the Ohio Historical Society. In addition to manuscripts cited in the present study, the Inventory lists MIC 70 and MIC 108 (containing material from MSS 680), MSS 136, MSS 984, and AV 9.

14. Ohio Historical Society, MSS 680. This collection contains documents donated by Edgar B. Nixon (including the collection of Dr. H. A. Coleman, given to Edgar B. Nixon by Coleman's widow) and Richard L. Nixon on behalf of the Nixon family. Edgar B. and Richard L. Nixon were great-grandsons of Simon Beuter, whose journal entries feature prominently in this study.

15. The papers and printed material of the Jack and Pat Adamson Collection compose MSS 1276 AV of the Ohio Historical Society. Of particular (but not sole) importance for this study are the following sections: box 9, folders 11–18 (general correspondence, 1860–65); box 11 (Civil War papers); box 18, folder 7 (autobiography of Eugene B. Wright); and boxes 23 and 24 (Civil War letters and translations).

16. The Western Reserve Historical Society, MS 1663.

17. The materials at the Ohio Historical Society and at the Western Reserve Historical Society together provide a remarkably complete resource on Zoar's economic history for some future scholar of ambition. A good start from a business and operational perspective is David William Meyers' 1980 master's thesis, "The Machine in the Garden." A comprehensive *economic* history of Zoar, however, is sadly overdue.

18. My translations of the Adamson papers appear throughout the files of MSS 1276 AV, but especially in boxes 11, 23, and 24.

19. MSS 1276 AV, box 9, folder 20. For resources on education at Zoar, see Nixon, "The Society of Separatists of Zoar," ch. 5; Henry Lee Holshoy, "The Educational Opportunities of the German Separatists"; MSS 680, box 2, folder 7; and the shocking criticism of child-rearing practices in Zoar by David L. Sylvan (i.e., Silvan) in his brief diary in MSS 680, box 3, folder 17.

20. MSS 110 AV, box 87, specifically folders 2 (1858–61) and 3 (1861–68).

21. MSS 1276 AV, box 9, folder 12. Andermann deserves a separate study. Among resources pertinent to such research would be documents in MSS 680, box 1, folder 9; and box 2, folder 2.

22. MSS 1276 AV, box 9, folder 15.

23. Morhart, *The Zoar Story*, 117.

24. Ibid.

25. Morhart, *The Zoar Story*, 119.

26. The first is Gustav Nieritz's *Alexander Menzikoff*; the second is Rudolph Leonhart's *Abenteuer eines deutschen Soldaten in Virginien*; and the third is a free translation of J. H. A. Bone's *The Indian Captive*, rendered in German as *Abenteuer unter den Indianern*. The volume is part of the Jack and Pat Adamson collection and can be paged at the Ohio Historical Society Archives and Library under the call number 833/N556a.

27. John S. C. Abbott, *Geschichte des Bürgerkrieges in Amerika*.

28. The journal is contained in MSS 680, Series II, box 4, folders 2 (including the period of the Civil War) and 3. They also compose MIC 70. A translation of Beuter's family history is in MSS 110 AV, box 2, folder 69.

29. Although a Swabian, like most Zoarites, Beuter was evidently a stickler for the use of standard German. See MSS 680, box 6, cards under the topic "Dialects." Beuter, a longtime school teacher in Zoar who had completed his schooling in Germany, no doubt felt it incumbent upon himself to model correct use of the German language.

30. MSS 110 AV, box 86, folder 1.

31. Fernandez, "Communal Communications"; see also Peter Hoehnle, "Communal Bonds."

32. MSS 110 AV, box 64, cash book 19, entries for September 7 and 9, 1861. The cash books pertinent to this study are MSS 110 AV, boxes 64 and 65, cash books 19–23.

33. MSS 110 AV, box 86, folder 1.

34. Donna DeBlasio's 1995 typescript "Zoar—Civil War Veterans" and the ever-expanding database "List of Persons Associated with the Zoar Community, 1817–1905" are both available for researchers at Zoar Village State Memorial and provide a wealth of personal information on the soldiers. Both have been incorporated into Steve Shonk's unsigned article "Glücklich Neujahr!"

35. MSS 110 AV, box 86, folder 1.

36. For the response of another Pietist communal society (the Inspirationists of the Amana Colonies) to "the Great Rebellion," see Hoehnle, "With Malice toward None."

37. MSS 1276 AV, box 9, folder 15.

38. Some of the documents without signatures are copies, others contain only part of an original text, and still others may have been intended to remain (at least nominally) anonymous.

39. MSS 1276 AV, box 9, folder 15.

40. Morhart, *The Zoar Story*, 117.

41. Ibid.

42. Morhart, *The Zoar Story*, 117–19.

43. The appended roster of Jacob Smith, *Camps and Campaigns of the 107th Regiment*, 240–314, provides an excellent, quick reference for the 107th Ohio Volunteer Infantry. For rosters of Ohio units, the benchmark work continues to be the Ohio Roster Commission, *Official Roster;* it is supplemented by the typescript (and subsequently microfilmed) *Alphabetical index.*

44. Morhart, *The Zoar Story,* 117; Ohio Roster Commission, *Official Roster.*

45. DeBlasio, "Zoar—Civil War Veterans"; the database, "List of Persons Associated with the Zoar Community, 1817–1905."

46. Shonk, "Glücklich Neujahr!"

47. There appears to be some confusion in the record between this John Breil whom Smith, *Camps and Campaigns,* 284, records as having entered the service August 22, 1862, served in Company F of the 107th Ohio Volunteer Infantry, and died August 12, 1863, in a rebel prison in Richmond, Virginia, and (John?) Simon Breil of Company B, 25th Ohio Volunteer Infantry, who served September 9, 1861, to October 3, 1865.

48. Burkhart enlisted September 30, 1864, and served in Company D, 25th Ohio Volunteer Infantry, until mustered out on July 15, 1865. "Magues" [*sic*] Burkhart is mentioned alongside his brother Anthony (Anton) in the Tuscarawas County Genealogical Society's *Biographical record of Civil War veterans,* 574.

49. Although apparently not a member of the Society, his 1860 departure from Zoar is noted in Beuter's final journal entry for 1861, one of his letters to an unnamed Zoar recipient is preserved, and Christian Rieker mentions him as serving in the 4th Ohio Volunteer Infantry.

50. Frederick Kücherer served in Company I of the 107th Ohio Volunteer Infantry from August 22, 1862, to July 10, 1865.

51. The Kuemmerle family name is associated with Zoar, though some members of the family did leave the Society. George served in Company A of the 107th Ohio Volunteer Infantry from August 6, 1862, to July 10, 1865.

52. Jacob Kuemmerle entered the service at the same time as George Kuemmerle and served in the same company, but he died February 7, 1863, at Brooks Station, Virginia.

53. John Kuemmerle entered the service at the same time as George and Jacob Kuemmerle and served in the same company, but he died May 2, 1863, in the Battle of Chancellorsville, Virginia.

54. Extant evidence suggests that Langlotz's wife was Friederika Rieker, who had left Zoar in 1860. Langlotz gave his address in his one extant letter to Zoar as "H. Langlotz / Musician, 18th U.S. Infantry Band." I have been unable to recover more detailed and useful information on this soldier. See also note 14 in the "Zoar's Other Volunteers and the Civil War" chapter of this volume.

55. Only DeBlasio, "Zoar—Civil War Veterans," associates Smith with Zoar; Smith served in Company F of the 107th Ohio Volunteer Infantry from September 5, 1862, to his death at Camp Delaware, Ohio, on October 13, 1862.

56. Lucas Strobel served in Company A of the 107th Ohio Volunteer Infantry from August 8, 1862, to his death on July 15, 1863, at Gettysburg, Pennsylvania, of wounds received on July 2 in the battle there.

57. A laborer at Zoar, Thumm was only 18 when he entered Company I of the 107th Ohio Volunteer Infantry on August 22, 1862. He was wounded July 1, 1863, at Gettysburg, but recovered and continued to serve until the conclusion of the war. Thumm's name appears in the correspondence of other Zoar soldiers. The post office records at Zoar indicate that Thumm was something of a reader and hence may have been inspired by what he read in various publications to consider enlisting.

58. There exists abundant and understudied documentation on the trade enterprises at Zoar; see for example MSS 110 AV, boxes 25–28.

59. Ohio Roster Commission, *Official Roster,* vol. 7, 782–84.

60. There is no lack of documentation on Zoar's musical heritage, though a comprehensive study still awaits the proper scholar. John Brunny and Huldreich Langlotz both served as army musicians. The only nonsectarian publication of the Zoar press was Haydn's *Die Schöpfung,* proof sheets, which are in MSS 680, box 3, folder 5. (Jacob) Albert Beuter assumed the directorship of the Bloomington Conservatory of Music in Bloomington, Illinois: MSS 680, box 3, folder 13. The sheet music for Frank Sylvan's first violin part in the Zoar String Band is in MSS 1276 AV, box 16, folder 1. Many other resources might be cited.

61. Unfortunately, Kern does not appear in the record of www.ohiohistory.org/resource/database/civilwar, the Ohio Historical Society Civil War Documents searchable database.

62. Morhart, *The Zoar Story,* 119. Among the works on this prison, see William Marvel, *Andersonville.*

63. See entries for August 22 and August 25, 1862, in MSS 110 AV, box 64, cash book 20.

64. MSS 1276 AV, box 18, folder 7. Documents by and about Eugene B. Wright are contained in MS 1276 AV, box 9, folder 14; box 18, folder 7; and (in the translated materials) boxes 23 and 24. Scattered references to Wright appear MSS 1276 AV, Civil War Papers, box 11.

65. For the local perspective, including the role of Tuscarawas County resident Charles Mueller, who took the unit to Cleveland and became lieutenant colonel of the regiment, see John Brandt Mansfield, *The History of Tuscarawas County,* esp. 450–53.

66. For the role of Sigel's (Siegel's) personal charisma in recruiting German Americans to the 107th Ohio Volunteer Infantry, see Smith, *Camps and Campaigns,* 9. There is no dearth of information on the song. Some of the many Web sites featuring lyrics and tune include www.enter.net/~alw/45th/sigel and www.usgennet.org/usa/mo/county/ stlouis/mitsigel.

67. Smith, *Camps and Campaigns,* 14.

68. Nixon, "The Society of Separatists of Zoar," ch. 10, goes into great detail about the political leanings of Zoar over time.

69. Smith, *Camps and Campaigns*, 20, 175.

70. The incident is reported in Morhart, *The Zoar Story*, 119. One of truly numerous patriotic documents held at Zoar was the poem to Lincoln "Der Unterdrückten warst du ein Befreier" (You were a Liberator of the Oppressed), MSS 1276 AV, box 18, folder 8, cited here as an example of the idealism fostered in the hearts and minds of many Zoarites.

71. Blicksenderfer, widow of Jacob Blicksenderfer (who along with Joseph C. Hance helped prepare the final will and testimony of Joseph M. Bimeler [Bäumeler]), had been the personal beneficiary of Zoar largesse at least since early 1860. See her letter dated January 20, 1860, in MSS 680, box 1, folder 4; the letter cited here is in MSS 680, box 1, folder 2; the note from Deardorff and Demuth is in MSS 680, box 2, folder 2. The name Peter Deardorf(f) also appears in the commercial records of the Society.

72. Webber, "Jakob Sylvan's Preface," esp. 122.

73. The draft English version addresses him as "His Excellency David Tod, Governor of Ohio." In the German version, this opening is missing altogether.

74. The document, MSS 1276 AV, box 11, folder 2, exists in a German version dated simply 1862. A draft English version and a final petition to Governor Tod (cited here), MSS 1276 AV, box 11, folder 3, show only cosmetic differences. The English draft is marked "Concept of a petition to Gov. Todd [*sic*]" in ink, and later in pencil (erroneously) "1861." The final version of the document is dated "Zoar, O. Sept. 23, 1862," in the script of the final copyist.

75. The other signers were (here in alphabetical order): Jacob Ackermann Jr., Mathias Beehler, Bernhard Beiter, Raymond Beiter, Simon Beiter, Levi Bimeler, Clemenz Breil, Conrad Breymaier, William Ehlers, Jacob Fritz, Samuel Harr, Fredrich Heid, Charles Kappel, Godfrey Kappel, Godfrey Lenz, Michael Miller, John Petermann, Martin Rauschenberger, Jacob Rieker, John Rieker, Benjamin Ruof, John G. Ruof, David Silvan, Francis Strobel, John Sturm, Christian Weebel, and Christian Zimmermann. Exact identification of certain individuals is problematic since, in some instances, others in Zoar had the same or a similar names.

76. In the Society of Separatists of Zoar, the "first-class membership" was the initial level of membership, whereas the "second-class membership" was in fact the level of full membership.

77. Though dated in parts, Nixon, "The Society of Separatists of Zoar," still gives the most nuanced treatment of the rise and decline of the Society and certainly does so with respect to the use of primary sources.

78. Nixon, "The Society of Separatists of Zoar," ch. 6.

79. MSS 110 AV, box 64, cash book 20.

80. Ibid.

81. Might the items given "earlier" refer to mementos such as the hand-copied text of Psalm 91 to which Morhart refers in *The Zoar Story,* 117? We do know that one recipient of a box of items sent from Zoar to Cleveland was Eugene B. Wright (whose experience is considered in detail in the following chapter). See correspondence of David L. Silvan and Union Line Express agent H. H. Eddis, MSS 680, box 1, folder 9.

82. MSS 1276 AV, box 9, folder 15.

83. Woolson's letter, in English, is preserved in MSS 680, box 2, folder 2.

84. MSS 1276 AV, box 11, folder 4.

85. MSS 680, box 6, cards under the heading "Civil War," cites a letter dated October 4, 1862, from Harry (Heinrich, Henry) Andermann, of New Philadelphia, to (Christian) Weebel (Wiebel): "I send you herewith a paper from Columbus . . . [regarding] the Proclamation of Gov. Tod, which relates to you, as a 'religious society opposed to the duties of war' [and] which clearly states your case as subject to Penalty of $200.00. I have been to see Commissioner Stockwell . . . [and] you are to come here on Wednesday to pay him $200.00 for each of your men." This letter is not in MSS 680, box 2, folder 2, as one might expect, nor elsewhere, as far as I can ascertain. I have not been able to find reference to Governor Tod's response, much less the original "Proclamation." Among sources checked were the gubernatorial records on microfilm GR 3951 of the Ohio Historical Society Library, and the inventory of Gov. David Tod's papers, January 13, 1862, to January 11, 1864, prepared by the Work Projects Administration and on deposit at the Ohio Historical Society Library. The latter resource is especially valuable because it contains references to some records that are no longer extant.

86. MSS 110 AV, box 64, cash book 20. There appears to be some confusion in the record as to when, or even on how many occasions, the Society paid for Bimeler and Ruof.

87. MSS 680, box 2, folder 2, letters of October 7 and (esp.) of October 14, 1862.

88. MSS 680, box 6, under the heading "Civil War." The report, from an unidentified newspaper, is dated Harrisburg, October 11, and hence might have been in Zimmermann's possession in time to send along with his letter of October 14, 1862. An accompanying typewritten note (by Edgar B. Nixon?) states, "Comments on the progress of the war occur in letters of the Society agents [such as Zimmermann] to the Society. Sometimes newspaper clippings are enclosed. Attached clipping mailed *from Philadelphia*" (my italics).

89. MSS 1276 AV, box 11, folder 6.

90. Kathleen Fernandez was kind enough to call this letter to my attention. MSS 1276, box 9, folder 15.

91. On November 28, 1844, Jacob David Seyfang petitioned the Senate and House of Representatives General Assembly of the State of Ohio for a change of name from Seyfang to Silvan (sometimes later spelled Sylvan). The reason given by the family for the change was that "their said name has in their Mother-Language, German, an awkward and unbecoming meaning, and in the Language of this Country has rather no meaning at all." In the Swabian dialect spoken by virtually all Zoarites, Seyfang sounds like "sow grab" and no doubt had the potential to spawn some "unbecoming" remarks from time to time. MSS 110 AV, box 84, folder 1.

92. MSS 680, box 1, folder 22. For background on the lawsuit, see Randall, "The Society of Separatists of Zoar," 23–31; and Nixon, "The Society of Separatists of Zoar," ch. 9. Additional records appear in MSS 110 AV, box 3. As I was preparing the manuscript of this study, Kathleen M. Fernandez was preparing

her presentation for the 2005 Communal Studies Association Conference, which sheds important new light on this topic.

93. MSS 1276 AV, box 9, folder 16, letters of February 25, 1863, and March 5, 1863. As always, Woolson's correspondence is in English.

94. MSS 1276 AV, box 11, folder 11.

95. Ohio Roster Commission, *Official Roster,* vol. 7, 782, reports Kappel's death on June 13, 1863; one also encounters other dates, some as much as one year later. For a discussion of the date of Kappel's death, see Shonk, "Glücklich Neujahr!" A more substantive issue that is not entirely clear is the cause of death. According to information cited in Shonk, it was "disease," and DeBlasio, "Zoar—Civil War Veterans," specifies the cause as pneumonia. Less clear from the extant record is the degree to which the wounds Kappel evidently received at the Battle of Gettysburg were the ultimate cause of his fatal disease.

96. William Bimeler copied and compiled the records of births, deaths, some membership data, and a smattering of other notabilia. This documentation is preserved in MSS 110 AV, box 2, folder 64. He dates it "Abgeschrieben (copied) January 17, 1908. William A. Bäumler Zoar, Ohio." Not all material is presented consecutively, though when one becomes familiar with the book, one can scan for births between 1834 and 1898 and deaths between 1832 and 1905 (including the cholera deaths of 1834).

97. MSS 1276 AV, box 11, folder 9.

98. MSS 110 AV, box 96, folder 2.

99. There are twenty-five numbered spaces for signatures; in alphabetical order, the twenty-four signers were (with names spelled as in the document) Christian Ackerman Jr., Jacob Ackermann Jr., Simon Beiter, Augustus Bimeler, Clemens Breil, Friedrich Breil, John Breymaier, John C. Breymaier, Jacob Brunny, Jacob Bühler, Magnus Burkhart, Mathäus Dischinger, John Grötzinger, Samuel Harr, Louis H. Heid, Charles Kappel, Adam Kümmerle, John Notter, John Petermann, John Rieker, Benjamen Rouf, David L. Silvan, John Sturm, and Christian Zimmerman.

100. MSS 680, box 2, folder 2.

101. The receipts were issued for payment by the following individuals (again, with names spelled as in the document): Christian Ackerman Jr., Jacob Ackerman, Augustus Bimeler, Levi Bimeler, Simon Biter, Clemens Brile, Frederic Brile, Conrad Breymeier, John Brymeier, Jacob Bruny, Jacob Buhler, Sebastian Burkhart, Charles Capple, Mathias Dishinger, John Grotzinger, Samuel Harr, Lewis Haid, Adam Kimmerle, John Notter, John Peterman, John Rieker, Benjamin Ruof, Christian Ruof, John Sturm, and Christian Zimmerman. The expense to the Society of $50 for fines is recorded in MSS 110 AV, box 64, cash book 22, entry for September 25, 1863.

102. MSS 680, box 1, folder 9, and MSS 110 AV, box 64, cash book 22, respectively.

103. MS 1663, container 2, folder 20.

104. MSS 1276 AV, box 9, folder 16, letters from Cleveland to "Mr. Rouf [*sic*]" dated September 21 and October 8, 1863. I thank Kathleen Fernandez for pointing out that Woolson manufactured these stoves.

105. I am indebted to Kathleen Fernandez for drawing to my attention the entries for Woolson, Hitchcock & Carter in the Cleveland City Directories for 1861–62 and 1863–64. The entry is under the name of the company in J. H. Williston, *J. H. Williston & Co.'s Directory of the City of Cleveland* (Cleveland: Ben Franklin Printing, 1861); and Andrew Boyd, *Boyd's Cleveland Directory, and Cuyahoga Co. Business Directory, to which is prefixed an appendix of much useful information, 1863–64* (Cleveland: Ingham, 1863).

106. See MS 1663, esp. container 1, folders 3, 4, and 7. Zoar had a long history of speculative investment that deserves detailed investigation beyond what is possible in this study.

107. MSS 680, box 1, folder 9. The Western Reserve Historical Society MS 1663, container 1, folder 3, is replete with correspondence between the Society and Merchants Bank of Massillon and its successor, First National Bank of Massillon. During November and December 1863, the Society and the bank corresponded almost as quickly as turnabout mail service permitted.

108. Shonk, "Glücklich Neujahr!" 2.

109. MSS 680, box 2, folder 2.

110. MSS 110 AV, box 64, cash book 22; and MSS 110 AV, box 2, folder 64, 79.

111. MSS 680, box 1, folder 10, letters of April 4, 6, and 10, 1864.

112. Evidently there was a certain amount of rather routine advancing of funds to Beuter, with subsequent settlement. MSS 110 AV, box 65, cash book 23, entry for June 23, 1864, shows that Simon Beuter refunded $120.96 "bounty-money advanced by Z[oar] Society in 1862" and that this was "the second & last portion f[rom] 1862."

113. MSS 1276 AV, box 11, folder 11.

114. MSS 110 AV, box 65, cash book 23.

115. MSS 1276 AV, box 9, folder 19.

116. MSS 680, box 2, folder 2. The receipts, dated March 4, 1867, are numbered 40,976–40,980.

EUGENE B. WRIGHT

1. Wright's letters are contained in MSS 1276 AV, box 9, folder 14. Some of the unidentified material in MSS 1276 AV, box 11, folders 4, 5, and 11, is probably by Wright; his (auto)biography is in MSS 1276 AV, box 18, folder 7, where it had been kept in a yellow envelope marked (in English) "Biography of my friend Eugene B. Wright." Wright wrote in both German and English. I have indicated which items were originally in English.

2. Nixon, "The Society of Separatists of Zoar," ch. 8, explains the Zoar practice

of accepting and raising foundlings. It is intriguing to speculate that Eugene B. Wright's father might have been David Wright, who was briefly affiliated with the Society in 1831: MSS 110 AV, box 2, folder 41. A letter contained in MSS 680, box 1, folder 2, and drawn to my attention by Kathleen M. Fernandez, may eventually help to shed light on the details of Eugene B. Wright's birth. A certain Anthony Wright wrote from Saint Louis, Missouri, to Lewis F. Birk at Zoar on June 10, 1850. The preceding September, Anthony had visited Zoar and had been allowed to see the young Eugene. Anthony declares that the father is willing to acknowledge Eugene as his son, and (Anthony) asks that the name currently in use, Eugene B. Russell—a fabrication by the mother, according to Anthony—be changed to Eugene B. Wright. Eugene's father is said to possess some six to seven thousand dollars and would be inclined to "make provision for [Eugene] and doubtless will do it in the name of Wright." The mother, whose identity appears to be a recent disclosure to members of the Zoar community, "doubtless would object to [Eugene] assuming [the father's] proper name . . . fearing that it might be a source of gratification to the father." Anthony suggests that Eugene be trained as a miller since that will "give him a better opportunity to learn the habits of the world and especially a better chance to learn the English language." Anthony mentions gifts given to Eugene during the last visit, offers moral admonitions to the lad in this letter, and asks whether the father or his friends might eventually visit Eugene. Anthony's relationship to Eugene's father remains unclear. A note indicates that the letter was received on June 18, and an answer of undisclosed content sent June 20, 1850. Much of the context of the letter remains unclear.

3. This David Silvan was of course not the much younger David L. Silvan born in 1839.

4. Despite his unspecified misconduct, Heinrich Hiessrich (Hißrich) continued to appear in Zoar correspondence. Heinrich's mother, Margaretha Hißrich, wrote to David Sylvan from Pittsburgh, Pennsylvania, on June 13, 1861, to report that Heinrich was no longer in Washington but rather in Alexandria, Virginia, helping to produce the Fifth Regiment's weekly newspaper, the *Pennsylvania Fifth*. Heinrich himself wrote to Silvan on December 2, 1866, to thank him for, among other things, "the barrel with dried fruit" that had arrived in time for the holiday celebrations. MSS 1276 AV, box 9, folders 12 and 19.

5. An item marked *Ve[r]gessene (Forgotten) Memento* 1865 in MSS 1276 AV, box 9, folder 18, may shed some light on Wright's social discomfort in Zoar. Not all allusions in the following text are entirely clear here, but this appears to be part of the controversy between Simon Beiter (Beuter) and (in all likelihood) Eugene B. Wright. If the date is 1865, and if the author was Wright, this "forgotten" document would then appear to have been "released" after "a decent interval" of about one year after Wright's death in early 1864. There is enough editing within the body of this letter to show that it was still in draft stage and may never have been sent. Perhaps the letter represented its author's private venting and was intentionally never sent to Simon Beuter. The reference to "Jakob" is evidently to (Jacob)

Albert Beuter, who left Zoar for the Harmonists and eventually entered the world at large as a musician and music educator. See above, note 60, for introduction.

Simon Beiter!

I cannot be satisfied, by far, with what you have mandated in writing [vorgeschrieben] for me; hence, I wish either to be convinced of various sentences [or points], or to see you retract them.

You claimed that others and I are haughty youngsters who look down on others and wish to take the rule. But prove to me that I did not always respond [to you] in a becoming manner, or that I have not done so to any other member of the Society. If you can demonstrate that, I shall gladly retreat as a "haughty youngster" [translator's quotation marks].

Further, you say that I do not always have to defend my [circle of] friendship so much. At the same time, you do indeed defend your own. But also in this matter, I wish you could point to one single instance where I defended my friends, except in precisely this [matter]. And I believe that I have a right to do so, for it is not right, for Jakob [extended illegible matter] has done more service for the Society here than have Jakob and I. To presume [to say] that he should bang out [herumklappern] his piano exercises on a board with his [free fingers?] (that certainly do not come from idleness), that is too presumptuous.

In general, it amazes me that you come to me concerning [crossed out in MS: Jakob's letter] the Society, as that does not at all concern me. His [Jakob's] opinion about it all concurs expressly with my own, which I shall express openly when the rest [is] past.

I do not like it, and you yourself say that you don't like it, and Jakob also knows that it isn't right. Otherwise he would not have pointed out [to me]: Do not let anyone read this letter!

You accuse me further (though not directly, but indeed indirectly) as though I wanted to impede Jacob [no surname given] behind his back. I believe you have shown no cause for this accusation.

That I expressed my opinion that the letters displeased me is no cause [for accusation] on your part, for you [illegible] have done the same [illegible]. I supposedly caused general alarm by all this, and then I would peacefully [illegible] myself guilty, but not so.

I made accusations to you about Jacob going to Bolivar . . . and I take that back because it does not concern me at all. (For, I abide by Dr. Franklin's principle: keep your mouth and fingers free of whatever does not pertain to you.)

Furthermore, I made allegations to you that Jacob had embarrassed the Society. What I really meant is that he made our music and instrument laughable. (That was more of a spontaneous remark.) That, too, I take back completely, for the same reason that that is of absolutely no concern to me.

If you find these lines worthy of an answer, please respond to the first two sentences [or points], and I would like to know that these points have been proven or retracted.

It is by far not my goal to [be contentious?], for I know my own faults only too well. But I also want my rights.

6. MSS 1276 AV, box 18, folder 7.

7. MSS 1276 AV, box 9, folder 14.

8. MSS 1276 AV, box 9, folder 36.

9. MSS 1276 AV, box 11, folder 4. Though unsigned, the handwriting and stylistic features are those of Wright.

10. Four parts were eventually printed: Joseph Michael Bimeler (Bäumeler), *Die wahre Separation, oder Die Wiedergeburt.*

11. MSS 1276 AV, box 18, folder 7.

12. MSS 1276 AV, box 11, folder 4.

13. Ibid.

14. MSS 1276 AV, box 18, folder 7.

15. MSS 1276 AV, box 11, folder 4.

16. MSS 1276 AV, box 11, folder 5.

17. MSS 680, box 1, folder 9. The inventory for this folder lists and describes a number of letters from Andermann to Zoar, particularly to Christian Wiebel (Weebel); see also MSS 680, box 2, bolder 2.

18. MSS 1276 AV, box 9, folder 14.

19. Ibid.

20. Ibid.

21. Ibid.

22. Ibid.

23. Ibid.

24. Ibid.

25. Ibid.

26. Ibid.

27. MSS 1276 AV, box 9, folder 16.

28. Ibid.

29. MSS 1276 AV, box 9, folder 14.

30. MSS 1276 AV, box 9, folder 36. It is a curious fact that the extant papers associated with Wright contain an undated and unsigned item in what appears to be his handwriting, taking a stance that clearly glorifies the soldier as an instrument of justice who relies upon the mercy of God. In some ways, it stands in antithesis to the statement just cited. If this document was indeed part of Wright's papers, did he keep this as an example of what he opposed? Or did he actually admire the figure of the soldier that he knew he could not become? Did he actually hear this speech or know the officer who delivered it? Or was it even a real speech or perhaps merely a genre piece? One can only speculate on the reasons for preserving this document, now in MSS 1276 AV, box 11, folder 12.

Speech to the Soldiers before the Encounter

Esteemed and beloved fellow-warriors for our oppressed and so preciously purchased fatherland! In the name of God, let us now begin to chastise our enemies and the destroyers of the general peace and happiness, to bring them again into the earlier relationship with us, and to seek thereby again to crown the United States with unity and peace, so that happiness and blessing may blossom, and that the Republic may emerge the victor with the star-spangled banner at the forefront.

Thanks be to our venerable forefathers and friends of the fatherland, who had to purchase for us the priceless blessing of freedom at such a price, and do battle with so many almost unconquerable enemies. As their sons, we ought now to lay our hands upon our bosoms and look to the honor of our fatherland, for it all depends upon the love of the fatherland and on the courage of those on whom the joy and happiness of our land depends. As millions await with fearful heart the outcome, it would be a disgrace for us if we did not wish to sacrifice our life for the general good!

Hence I admonish you once again, perhaps for the last time: Fight for the blessing of God and make yourselves worthy to stand in the ranks of those who have offered up their lives in order to achieve the good of many millions. Commend your souls to God and let each ask the one who alone can help to strengthen us in the moment when our life and the future good of the country is at stake.

Think of our forefathers and of our eternally beloved Washington.

God, show us your might, that we might always and only trust in you alone, if it is your will to allow us to live longer.

With this, depending on the might of God and on your courage and love of the fatherland, we wish with noble intentions in our hearts, to seize the enemy in . . . obedience to [our] superiors . . . with God determining our further fate. I am your fellow combatant for freedom.

31. MSS 1276 AV, box 9, folder 36.

32. Both Simon Beuter and William Bimeler record the hymn for Wright's funeral service as "Christe mein Leben" and the text as the 24th Meditation (Betrachtung) in Gerhard Tersteegen's *Blumengärtlein*.

33. MSS 110 AV, box 7, entry for April 1, 1864.

34. MSS 110 AV, box 64, cash book 22.

ZOAR'S OTHER VOLUNTEERS AND THE CIVIL WAR

1. Rieker's letters are contained in MSS 110 AV, box 96, folder 1.

2. Smith, *Camps and Campaigns,* 21. While Smith says that the funeral was "probably the first duty of our kind performed by members of our Regiment," Rieker indicates that there had been others. Perhaps Smith is reporting on the

first incident where the 107th Ohio officiated, whereas Rieker may simply be indicating that this is not the first seen during his tour of duty.

3. The stationary depicts, on the left, a woman holding a shield and an American flag with the words "for the union," and on the right, an eagle above the word "Iowa," crossed out by hand and corrected to "Ohio." Under the woman: C. Magnus, 12 Frankfurt Street. N.Y.

4. The stationary depicts, on the left, an eagle on a shield, and on the right the U.S. Senate in session. Under the eagle and shield: Chas. Magnus, 12 Frankfurt Street. N.Y.

5. Jähle, in fact, appears in the account books after the war as a resident of Wooster who continued to do business with the Society.

6. Major General Joseph Hooker, as Rieker may have remembered him, appears in a portrait in the collection of the Library of Congress, Prints and Photographs Division, LC-B8172-6385. The portrayal of Hooker in Smith, *Camps and Campaigns,* esp. 53, provides a valuable complement to Rieker's correspondence.

7. According to the database "List of Persons Associated with the Zoar Community, 1817–1905," and Simon Beuter's summarizing comments for the year 1861, we know that Friederika (Friederike) Rieker (Riker) was born in 1839 and that she became a first-class member of the Society in 1859, while still nineteen years of age, but left the Society in 1861. Perhaps she left because of an intention to marry Huldreich Langlotz. The couple apparently lived for at least a while in Columbus and maintained good relations with the Rieker family and with other Zoarites.

8. See for example the detailed account in Smith, *Camps and Campaigns,* 61–62.

9. Smith, *Camps and Campaigns,* 86.

10. MSS 110 AV, box 96, folder 1.

11. In the records, one finds various forms of Mary or Anna Maria as the sister's given name, and Ruof or Rouf as her married surname.

12. The Zoarites were from Swabia, where to this day Teigwaren (dough products for cooking) continue to enjoy popularity. Typically, Riwele are made from eggs, flour, and perhaps a bit of shortening. The mass of dough is crumbled into small pieces and allowed to dry. Cooking re-plumps the dough and gives it the desired texture.

13. MSS 110 AV, box 96, folder 1.

14. The roster for this unit given by www.usregulars.com/library lists three musicians with the name Langlotz; none have the first name Huldrich, though all three have a first name (e.g., Kuldrich) that may be a misspelling of this soldier's name.

15. Simon Beuter and William Bimeler, in their respective works, report the passing of Rieker in identical detail. The funeral service is recorded in MSS 1276 AV, box 1, folder 45.

16. The hymn was "Gott du hast verschiedene Ruthen"; the basis of the meditation consisted of the 560th set of rhymes (*Schlussreim*) in the *Geistliches Blumengärtlein* ("Little Garden of Spiritual Flowers") anthology by Gerhard Tersteegen. The Tersteegen anthology was one of the fundamental textual corpora of the Zoar Pietists.

17. The first letter is in MSS 680, box 2, folder 2; all others are drawn from MSS 1276 AV, box 11, folder 8.

18. A short accompanying scrap of paper about (divinely appointed?) limits of the power of Napolion [*sic*] appears unrelated to this letter. There is a small yellow envelope addressed to "Christ. Ruof Esq / care Zoar Society / Zoar / Ohio"; the impressed return address is "S. Buhrer / Mf'r. of / Buhrer's Gentian Bitters / 64 & 66 / Merwin St / Cleveland." I appreciate Kathleen Fernandez's pointing out that Stephen Buhrer, like Wright, was raised by the Separatists, left Zoar for Cleveland, and eventually became that city's mayor. His picture appears in Fernandez, *A Singular People,* 146.

19. Brunny's letters are preserved in MSS 110 AV, box 96, folder 1 (as is this one), and in MSS 1276 AV, box 11, folder 7 (the letters of December 28, 1862, and of July 28, 1864). This letter, written at Camp Wallace (near Covington, Kentucky), features an imposing portrait of Ambrose Everett Burnside, simply labeled "Burnside."

20. Smith, *Camps and Campaigns,* 16, dates this march as September 27.

21. For more on this lowly staple of the military diet, see Smith, *Camps and Campaigns,* 39–40. It is probably reasonable to suppose that Christian Rieker, in prison, was nevertheless overjoyed for the crackers that his sister sent him.

22. MSS 1276 AV, box 11, folder 7.

23. See Fernandez, "Communal Communications," 9. The cider mill was being constructed with assistance from the Harmonists.

24. MSS 110 AV, box 96, folder 1.

25. MSS 1276 AV, box 11, folder 7.

26. The letters of June 6, 1863, and June 2, 1864, are in MSS 1276 AV, box 11, folder 10; the note of March 3, 1864, is in MSS 1276 AV, box 9, folder 17.

27. For the few details that we know about Strobel, see Steve Shonk, "Glücklich Neujahr!" 4.

28. MSS 1276 AV, box 11, folder 10.

29. MSS 1276 AV, box 9, folder 17.

30. See the cash books in MSS 110 AV, boxes 64 and 65.

31. MSS 1276 AV, box 11, folder 10.

32. MSS 1276 AV, box 9, folder 19. Ben Feucht corresponded with David L. Silvan about the health of Silvan's wife, Paulina.

THE AFTERMATH

1. *Harper's New Monthly Magazine* 41 (July 1870): 282–85. Constance Fenimore Woolson was the daughter of Charles J. Woolson and her great-uncle was James Fenimore Cooper. Her stories "Wilhelmina" and "Solomon" in the collection *Castle Nowhere: Lake Country Sketches* also draw heavily on observations of her life at Zoar. Though many of her works deal with the South and Reconstruction, one cannot help wondering to what extent her stays in Zoar may also have shaped her thinking in one way or another about issues of war and its impact.

2. See the letter of Constance Fenimore Woolson to David L. Silvan in MSS 1276 AV, box 9, folder 25. A paper that merits far wider attention and—I hope someday—publication is Kathleen Fernandez's "'The Happy Valley.'"

3. Steve Shonk was kind enough to share a copy of this document with me. The hymn was "Mein treuer Hirt, wie komm' ich doch hinüber," and the basis of meditation consisted of the 565th *Schlußreim* (rhymed verse) in Gerhard Tersteegen's *Blumengärtlein*. This funeral sermon is one of the texts that formed a basis for Philip E. Webber, "Formulaic Patterns in Zoar Funeral Orations."

4. For photographic documentation of the parade, as well as of centennial exhibit items related to the Civil War, enter the search term "Grand Army of the Republic" at www.ohiohistory.org/etcetera/exhibits/ohiopix/.

5. The dates of death are taken from the database maintained at Zoar Village State Memorial. For the accounts of these soldiers, see Morhart, *The Zoar Story*, 117–19.

Select Bibliography

ARCHIVES AND MANUSCRIPT COLLECTIONS

Jack and Pat Adamson Collection (1709–1975). MSS 1276 AV Ohio Historical Society, Columbus.

"List of Persons Associated with the Zoar Community, 1817–1905." Zoar Village State Memorial, Ohio.

Nixon Family Papers. MSS 680. Ohio Historical Society, Columbus.

Records of the Society of Separatists of Zoar, 1817–1927 (1817–1873). Microfilm edition. MS 1663. Western Reserve Historical Society Library, Cleveland, Ohio.

Society of Separatists of Zoar Records, 1811–1946. MSS 110 AV. Ohio Historical Society, Columbus.

Tod, David. Inventory of gubernatorial papers January 13, 1862, to January 11, 1864. Ohio Historical Society Library. Journal-style entries to complement this are on microfilm GR 3951 of the Ohio Historical Society Library, Columbus.

PUBLISHED SOURCES

Abbott, John S. C. *Geschichte des Bürgerkrieges in Amerika.* . . . Trans. Julius Würzburger and Georg Dietz. Norwich, Conn.: H. Bill, 1863-66. Originally published as *The History of Civil War in America: Comprising a Full Account of the Origin and Progress of the Rebellion* (Springfield, Mass.: G. Bill, 1863–66).

Amana Church Society. *Davidisches Psalter-Spiel der Kinder Zions: oder, Sammlung von alten und neuen auserlesenen Geistes-Gesängen. Allen wahren heilsbegierigen Seelen und Säuglingen der Weisheit, insonderheit aber denen Gemeinden des Herrn zum gesegneten Gebrauch mit Fleiss zusammen getragen, nebst den dazu nöthigen und nützlichen Registern.* . . . Ebenezer, N.Y.; Amana, Iowa: Press of the Amana Church Society, continuous publication through 1910.

Bimeler (Bäumeler), Joseph Michael. *Die wahre Separation, oder Die Wiedergeburt: dargestellet in geistreichen und erbaulichen Versammlungsreden und Betrachtungen: besonders auf das gegenwärtige Zeitalter anwendbar: gehalten in der Gemeinde in Zoar im Jahr 1830 [1831, 1832, 1834] (The True Separation, or the Rebirth . . .).* 4 vols. Zoar, Ohio: Press of the Society of Separatists, 1856–60.

Bone, J. H. A. *Abenteuer unter den Indianern, oder Ina's Gefangenschaft unter den Wilden und ihre wunderbare Befreiung.* Pittsburgh, Pa.: J. M. Hoffmann, 1863. Originally published as *The Indian Captive: A Narrative of the Adventures and Sufferings of Matthew Brayton* (Cleveland, Ohio: Fairbanks, Benedict, 1860).

Coyle, William, ed. *Ohio Authors and Their Books: Biographical Data and Selective Bibliographies for Ohio Authors, Native and Resident, 1796–1950.* Cleveland, Ohio: World Publishing Company, 1962.

DeBlasio, Donna. "Zoar—Civil War Veterans." Typescript, Zoar Village State Memorial, Ohio.

Durnbaugh, Donald F. "'Strangers and Exiles': Assistance Given by the Religious Society of Friends to the Separatist Society of Zoar in 1817–1818." *Ohio History* 109 (2000): 71–92.

Fernandez, Kathleen M. "Communal Communications: Zoar's Letters to Harmony and Zoar." Presentation delivered at the 1984 Communal Studies Association Conference in Amana, Iowa.

———. "'The Happy Valley': Constance F. Woolson's View of Zoar." Paper presented at the 15th Annual Western Reserve Studies Symposium, 2000. Available online at http://www.case.edu/artsci/wrss/documents/Fernandez.pdf (accessed June 27, 2006).

———. "'The Society of Separatist of Zoar vs. . . . ': Zoar and the Courts." *Communal Societies* 26 (2006): 105–15.

———. *A Singular People: Images of Zoar.* Kent, Ohio: Kent State University Press, 2003.

Fritz, Eberhard. "Roots of Zoar, Ohio, in Early 19th Century Württemberg: The Separatist Group in Rottenacker and Its Circle." Pts. 1 and 2. *Communal Societies* 22 (2002): 27–44; 23 (2003): 29–44.

Grebner, Constantine. *"Die Neuner": eine Schilderung der Kreigsjahre des 9ten Regiments Ohio Vol. Infanterie, vom 17 April 1861 bis 7 June 1864.* Introd. Gustav Tafel. Cincinnati, Ohio: S. Rosenthal, 1897. Trans. and ed. by Fredrick Trautmann as *We Were The Ninth: A History of the Ninth Regiment, Ohio Volunteer Infantry April 17, 1861, to June 7, 1864* (Kent, Ohio: Kent State University Press, 1987).

Harper, Robert S. *Ohio Handbook of the Civil War.* Columbus: Ohio Historical Society for the Ohio Civil War Centennial Commission, 1961.

Hickman, Janet. *Zoar Blue.* 1978. Reprint, Columbus: Ohio Historical Society, 1998.

Hinds, William Alfred. *American Communities.* 1908. Reprint of rev. ed., Philadelphia, Pa.: Porcupine Press, 1975.

Hoehnle, Peter. "Communal Bonds: Contact between the Amana Society and Other Communal Groups, 1843–1932." *Communal Societies* 20 (2000): 59–80.

————. "With Malice toward None: The Inspirationist Response to the Civil War, 1860–65." *Communal Societies* 18 (1998): 62–80.

Holloway, Mark. *Heavens on Earth: Utopian Communities in America, 1680–1880.* 1951. Rev. ed., New York: Dover, 1966.

Holshoy, Henry Lee. "The Educational Opportunities of the German Separatists in the Communistic Settlement at Zoar, Ohio." Master's thesis, Kent State University, 1942.

Landis, George Butts. *The Society of Separatists of Zoar, Ohio.* From the annual report of the American Historical Association for 1898. Washington, D.C.: GPO, 1899.

Leonhart, Rudolph. *Abenteuer eines deutschen Soldaten in Virginien (Adventures of a German Soldier in Virginia).* Pittsburgh, Pa.: J. M. Hoffmann, 1863.

Mansfield, John Brandt. *The History of Tuscarawas County, Ohio.* Chicago: Warner, Beers, 1884.

Marvel, William. *Andersonville: The Last Depot.* Chapel Hill: University of North Carolina Press, 1994.

Meyers, David William. "The Machine in the Garden: The Design and Operation of the Separatist Society of Zoar." Master's thesis, Ohio State University, 1980.

Morhart, Hilda Dischinger. *The Zoar Story.* 3rd ed. Strasburg, Ohio: Gordon Printing, 1981.

Nieritz Gustav. *Alexander Menzikoff, oder die Gefahren des Reichtums (Alexander Menzikoff, or the Dangers of Wealth).* Pittsburgh, Pa.: Ernst Luft, n.d.

Nixon, Edgar Burkhard. "The Society of Separatists of Zoar." PhD diss., Ohio State University, 1933.

Nordhoff, Charles. *The Communistic Societies of the United States from Personal Visit and Observation.* 1875. Reprint with a new introd. by Mark Holloway. New York: Dover, 1966.

Ohio Roster Commission. *Official Roster of the Soldiers of the State of Ohio in the War of the Rebellion, 1861–1866.* 12 vols. Cincinnati: Wilstach, Baldwin; Akron, Ohio: Werner, 1886–95.

Ohio State Archaeological and Historical Society. *Zoar: An Ohio Experiment in Communalism.* 1970. Reprint, Columbus: Ohio Historical Society, 1987.

Randall, E[milius] O. "The Separatist Society of Zoar: An Experiment in Communism—from Its Commencement to Its Conclusion." *Ohio Archaeological and Historical Publications* 8 (1900): 1–105.

Reid, Whitelaw. *Ohio in the War: Her Statesmen, Generals, and Soldiers.* 1895. Reprint, Columbus, Ohio: Bergman Books, 1995.

Richter, Alexander. "Slavery, Abolitionism, and Race in Cincinnati's Antebellum German-Language Press and Emil Klauprecht's German-American Novel." Master's thesis, University of Cincinnati, 1999.

Robinson, Elwin C. "Heavenly Aspirations and Earthly Realities." *Timeline* 17/6 (2000): 2–25.

Rokicky, Catherine M. *Creating a Perfect World: Religious and Secular Utopias in Nineteenth-Century Ohio.* Athens: Ohio University Press, 2002.

Sammlung auserlesener geistlicher Lieder: zum gemeinschäftlichen Gesang und eigenen Gebrauch in Christlichen Familien (A Collection of Selected Spiritual Songs . . .). Zoar, Ohio: Press of the Society of Separatists, 1867

[Shonk, Steve.] "Glücklich Neujahr!" [Happy New Year!] *The Zoar Star* 9/44 (first quarter 1998): 1–5.

Smith, Jacob. *Camps and Campaigns of the 107th Regiment Ohio Volunteer Infantry, from August, 1862, to July, 1865*. 1910. Reprint, Navarre, Ohio: Indian River Graphics, 2000.

Specht, Neva Jean. "Constrained to Afford Them Countenance and Protection: The Role of the Philadelphia Friends in the Settlement of the Society of Separatists of Zoar." *Communal Societies* 24 (2004): 95–107.

Sutton, Robert P. *Communal Utopias and the American Experience: Religious Communities, 1732–2000*. Westport, Conn.: Praeger, 2003.

Tersteegen, Gerhard. *Geistliches Blumen-Gärtlein inniger Seelen: oder Kurze Schluss-Reimen, Betrachtungen und Lieder ueber allerhand Wahrheiten des inwendigen Christenthums*. Germantown, Pa.: Peter Leibert, 1791.

Tuscarawas County Genealogical Society. *Biographical record of Civil War veterans, Tuscarawas County, Ohio: Excerpts from Presidents, Soldiers, Statesmen*. 1892. Reprint, New Philadelphia, Ohio: Tuscarawas County Genealogical Society, 1990.

Watson, Carl, ed., et al. *Alphabetical index to official roster of the soldiers of the State of Ohio in the War of Rebellion (12 volumes) 1861–1866*. Cleveland: Works Progress Administration of Ohio, 1938.

Webber, Philip E. "Formulaic Patterns in Zoar Funeral Orations." Presentation delivered at the 1994 Communal Studies Association Conference in Oneida, New York, October 6–9, 1994.

————. "Jakob Sylvan's Preface to the Zoarite Anthology *Die wahre Separation: oder, die Wiedergeburt*, As an Introduction to Un(der)studied Separatist Principles." *Communal Societies* 19 (1999): 101–28.

————. "Simon Beuter's Journal as a Primary Source for Zoar History: Illustrated by Passages Dealing with the Passing of Zoar's Founding Leader, Joseph M. Bäumeler." *Communal Societies* 26 (2006): 117–34.

ONLINE SOURCES

German-language site on German Americans in the Civil War. www.bigcountry.de.

Ohio in the Civil War. www.ohiocivilwar.com.

Ohio Historical Society Civil War Documents (searchable database). www/ohiohistory.org/ resource/database/civilwar.

Index